STEPHEN BIESTY'S
INCREDIBLE
CROSS-SECTIONS

ILLUSTRATED BY
STEPHEN BIESTY

WRITTEN BY
RICHARD PLATT

Project Editor John C. Miles
Art Editor Richard Czapnik
Production Marguerite Fen
Managing Editor Ann Kramer
Art Director Roger Priddy

REVISED EDITION
Senior Editor Camilla Hallinan
Editor Sarah Edwards
US Editor Kayla Dugger
Assistant Editor Ankona Das
Art Editor Kit Lane
Assistant Art Editor Srishti Arora
Senior DTP Designer Sachin Singh
DTP Designers Dheeraj Singh, Bimlesh Tiwary
Pre-Production Manager Balwant Singh
Production Manager Pankaj Sharma
Producer, Pre-Production Gillian Reid
Senior Producer Mary Slater
Managing Editors Francesca Baines, Kingshuk Ghoshal
Managing Art Editors Philip Letsu, Govind Mittal
Publisher Andrew Macintyre
Publishing Director Jonathan Metcalf

This American Edition, 2019
First American Edition, 1995
Published in the United States by DK Publishing
1450 Broadway, 8th Floor, New York, New York 10018

Copyright © 1995, 2019 Dorling Kindersley Limited
DK, a Division of Penguin Random House LLC
19 20 21 22 23 10 9 8 7 6 5 4 3 2 1
001–314183–May/2019

A catalog record for this book is available
from the Library of Congress.
ISBN 978-1-4654-8389-8
Printed and bound in China

A WORLD OF IDEAS:
SEE ALL THERE IS TO KNOW

www.dk.com

CONTENTS

CASTLE 4

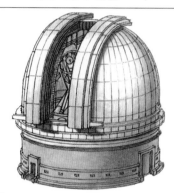

OBSERVATORY 6

GALLEON 8

OCEAN LINER 10

SUBMARINE 16

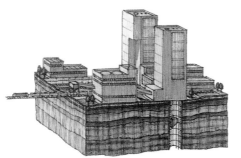

COAL MINE 18

TANK 20

OIL RIG 22

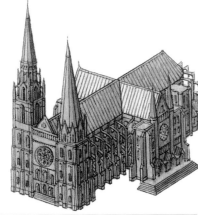

CATHEDRAL 24

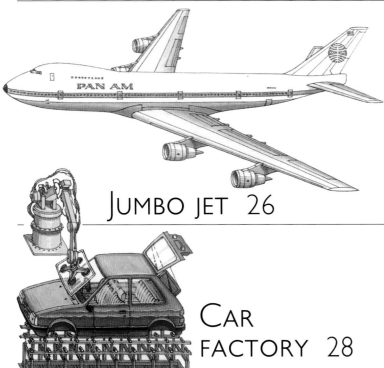

JUMBO JET 26

CAR FACTORY 28

HELICOPTER 30

OPERA HOUSE 32

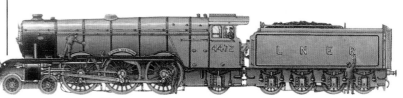

STEAM TRAIN 34

SUBWAY STATION 40

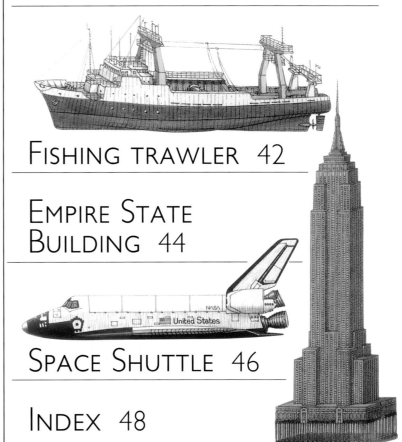

FISHING TRAWLER 42

EMPIRE STATE BUILDING 44

SPACE SHUTTLE 46

INDEX 48

Castle

Many 14th-century castles had thick outer walls, which enclosed a central open area.

Hundreds of years ago, life in Europe was dangerous, and wars were common. So powerful people built castles—strong homes where they could shelter from their enemies or launch attacks against them. Usually a nobleman or lord owned the castle. The king gave the lord land in return for soldiers to help fight wars. Tenants farmed the lord's land. In return for their labor, they earned enough to live on and were protected in wartime by the lord and his soldiers. Society inside the castle walls mirrored the world outside. The lord and his officials managed the castle and the lands around it. Below the officials there were priests, important servants, and soldiers. At the bottom of castle society were the most humble workers, such as laborers and the cesspit cleaner shown below.

Deadly fire
Narrow slits in the castle walls allowed archers to fire freely while protecting them from incoming arrows. The overhang at the top of the walls meant that the castle defenders could drop stones on attackers' heads to stop them climbing the walls.

Gatehouse
The only way into the castle was through the gatehouse. This was the weakest point in the castle wall. Defenders on the top of the wall fired arrows at attackers who got too close or threw boiling water down on them. The defenders could also lower a huge gate, called a portcullis, which trapped the attackers.

Getting inside
Capturing a castle was difficult. Attackers had to try to tunnel under the walls, trick the people inside, or lay siege and starve them out to gain access. Castles were an effective defense until the end of the 1300s, when gunpowder came into widespread use and attacking armies could blow holes in the strongest castle wall.

A moat point
Another defense was a water-filled trench called a moat, which surrounded the castle. The moat was a difficult hurdle for attackers, and also stopped them digging a tunnel under the walls. The road to the gatehouse crossed the moat by a hinged drawbridge that could be raised in seconds.

Doing time
Prisoners were locked up in an underground cell, called a dungeon. Oubliettes, or secret dungeons, got their name from the French word *oublier*, "to forget." Oubliettes were reserved for the most hated prisoners. Their captors locked them in the oubliette—and forgot about them!

Castle personalities

Cesspit cleaner   *Priest*   *Noble family*   *Jester*   *Knight*

Commander's quarters

Tiled roof

Castle guards

Food store

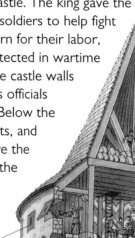

Portcullis

Drawbridge

On guard
This room was where the gate guards were stationed. They ate their meals here and warmed themselves by a basket of hot charcoal called a brazier.

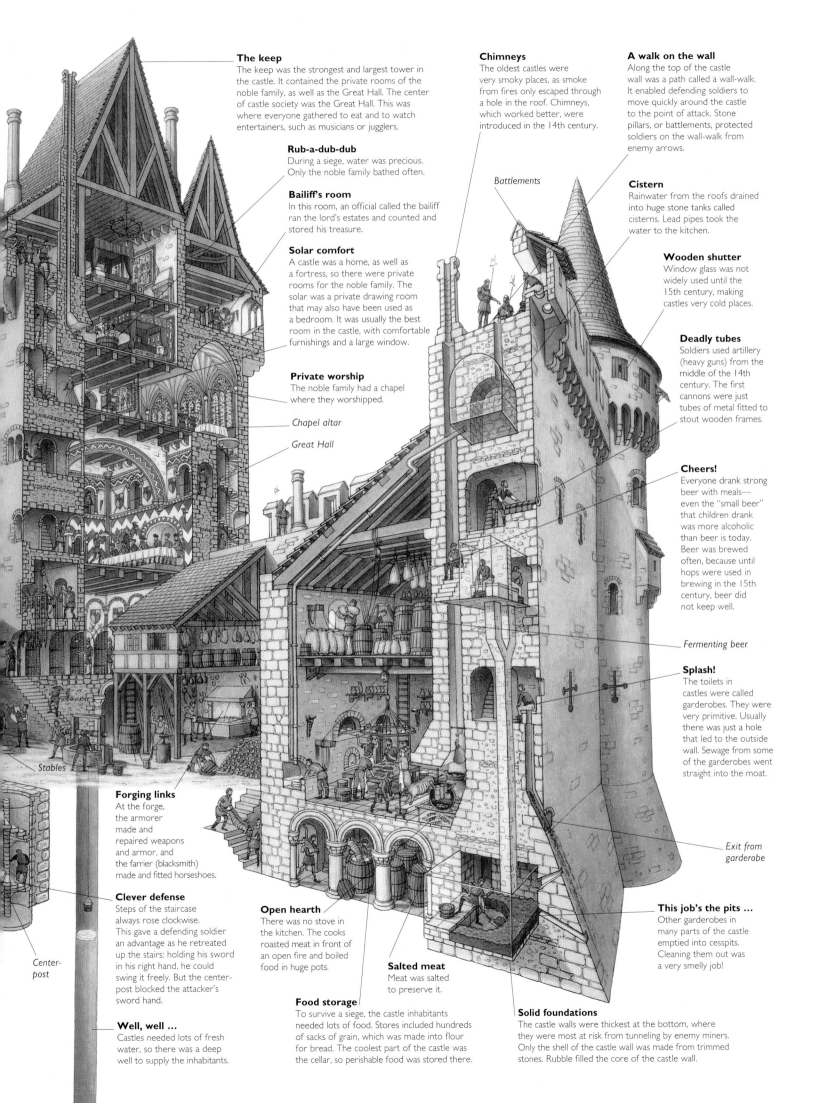

The keep
The keep was the strongest and largest tower in the castle. It contained the private rooms of the noble family, as well as the Great Hall. The center of castle society was the Great Hall. This was where everyone gathered to eat and to watch entertainers, such as musicians or jugglers.

Rub-a-dub-dub
During a siege, water was precious. Only the noble family bathed often.

Bailiff's room
In this room, an official called the bailiff ran the lord's estates and counted and stored his treasure.

Solar comfort
A castle was a home, as well as a fortress, so there were private rooms for the noble family. The solar was a private drawing room that may also have been used as a bedroom. It was usually the best room in the castle, with comfortable furnishings and a large window.

Private worship
The noble family had a chapel where they worshipped.

Chapel altar

Great Hall

Stables

Forging links
At the forge, the armorer made and repaired weapons and armor, and the farrier (blacksmith) made and fitted horseshoes.

Clever defense
Steps of the staircase always rose clockwise. This gave a defending soldier an advantage as he retreated up the stairs: holding his sword in his right hand, he could swing it freely. But the center-post blocked the attacker's sword hand.

Center-post

Well, well ...
Castles needed lots of fresh water, so there was a deep well to supply the inhabitants.

Open hearth
There was no stove in the kitchen. The cooks roasted meat in front of an open fire and boiled food in huge pots.

Food storage
To survive a siege, the castle inhabitants needed lots of food. Stores included hundreds of sacks of grain, which was made into flour for bread. The coolest part of the castle was the cellar, so perishable food was stored there.

Salted meat
Meat was salted to preserve it.

Chimneys
The oldest castles were very smoky places, as smoke from fires only escaped through a hole in the roof. Chimneys, which worked better, were introduced in the 14th century.

Battlements

Solid foundations
The castle walls were thickest at the bottom, where they were most at risk from tunneling by enemy miners. Only the shell of the castle wall was made from trimmed stones. Rubble filled the core of the castle wall.

A walk on the wall
Along the top of the castle wall was a path called a wall-walk. It enabled defending soldiers to move quickly around the castle to the point of attack. Stone pillars, or battlements, protected soldiers on the wall-walk from enemy arrows.

Cistern
Rainwater from the roofs drained into huge stone tanks called cisterns. Lead pipes took the water to the kitchen.

Wooden shutter
Window glass was not widely used until the 15th century, making castles very cold places.

Deadly tubes
Soldiers used artillery (heavy guns) from the middle of the 14th century. The first cannons were just tubes of metal fitted to stout wooden frames.

Cheers!
Everyone drank strong beer with meals— even the "small beer" that children drank was more alcoholic than beer is today. Beer was brewed often, because until hops were used in brewing in the 15th century, beer did not keep well.

Fermenting beer

Splash!
The toilets in castles were called garderobes. They were very primitive. Usually there was just a hole that led to the outside wall. Sewage from some of the garderobes went straight into the moat.

Exit from garderobe

This job's the pits ...
Other garderobes in many parts of the castle emptied into cesspits. Cleaning them out was a very smelly job!

Observatory

How far can you see? Pick up a telescope, and you can see mountains on the Moon nearly 248,550 miles (400,000 km) away. The Hale telescope at Mount Palomar, in California, is so powerful that it is never pointed at anything as close as the Moon. Instead, astronomers (people who study the stars) use it to look at far more distant objects in the night sky. The telescope's 200-in (5.1-m) wide mirror can detect stars too distant for our eyes to see. Some of these stars are so far away that their light takes millions of years to reach Earth. Looking at these stars is like looking into the past, because you are seeing them as they were millions of years ago.

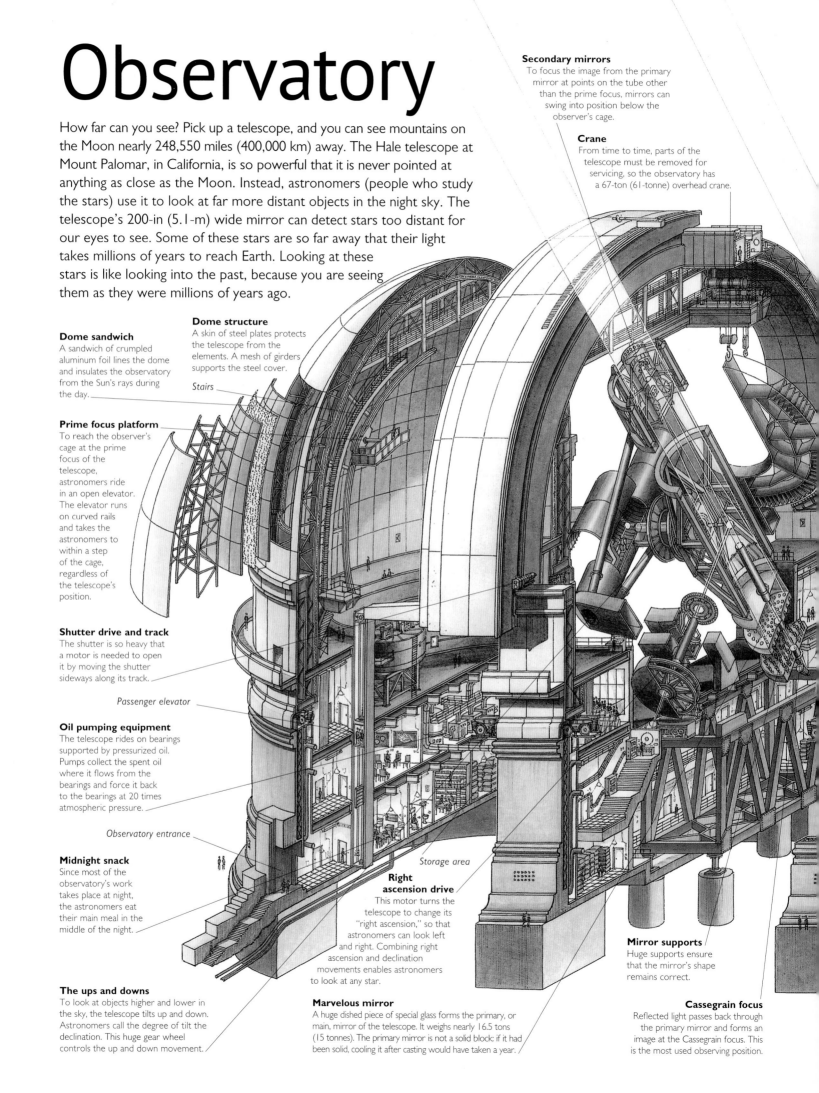

Secondary mirrors
To focus the image from the primary mirror at points on the tube other than the prime focus, mirrors can swing into position below the observer's cage.

Crane
From time to time, parts of the telescope must be removed for servicing, so the observatory has a 67-ton (61-tonne) overhead crane.

Dome structure
A skin of steel plates protects the telescope from the elements. A mesh of girders supports the steel cover.

Stairs

Dome sandwich
A sandwich of crumpled aluminum foil lines the dome and insulates the observatory from the Sun's rays during the day.

Prime focus platform
To reach the observer's cage at the prime focus of the telescope, astronomers ride in an open elevator. The elevator runs on curved rails and takes the astronomers to within a step of the cage, regardless of the telescope's position.

Shutter drive and track
The shutter is so heavy that a motor is needed to open it by moving the shutter sideways along its track.

Passenger elevator

Oil pumping equipment
The telescope rides on bearings supported by pressurized oil. Pumps collect the spent oil where it flows from the bearings and force it back to the bearings at 20 times atmospheric pressure.

Observatory entrance

Midnight snack
Since most of the observatory's work takes place at night, the astronomers eat their main meal in the middle of the night.

Storage area

Right ascension drive
This motor turns the telescope to change its "right ascension," so that astronomers can look left and right. Combining right ascension and declination movements enables astronomers to look at any star.

Mirror supports
Huge supports ensure that the mirror's shape remains correct.

The ups and downs
To look at objects higher and lower in the sky, the telescope tilts up and down. Astronomers call the degree of tilt the declination. This huge gear wheel controls the up and down movement.

Marvelous mirror
A huge dished piece of special glass forms the primary, or main, mirror of the telescope. It weighs nearly 16.5 tons (15 tonnes). The primary mirror is not a solid block: if it had been solid, cooling it after casting would have taken a year.

Cassegrain focus
Reflected light passes back through the primary mirror and forms an image at the Cassegrain focus. This is the most used observing position.

KEY FACTS

Dome diameter	• 135 ft (41.2 m)
Mirror diameter	• 200 in (5.1 m)
Tube length	• 54¾ ft (16.7 m)
Tube weight	• 595 tons (540 tonnes)

Dome shutter
The telescope "looks out" through a 29¾-ft (9.1-m) wide slot in the dome. When the observatory is not in use, two dome shutters cover the slot.

Shiny dome
Silver paint on the outside of the dome reflects the Sun's heat and helps the observatory stay cool.

Big eyes on the skies

The 200-in (5.1-m) reflecting telescope at Mount Palomar, in southern California, is named after George Ellery Hale (1868–1938), an American astronomer who helped plan and raise funds for the observatory. When the telescope was completed in 1948, it was the largest optical telescope in the world, and this record was broken only in 1976, when the Soviet Union brought a 236-in (6-m) reflecting telescope into use. The largest telescope in use today is the Gran Telescopio Canarias, on the island of La Palma, in the Canary Islands, Spain. Its mirror is an amazing 410 in (10.4 m) wide.

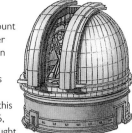

Field of view of telescope
The telescope gives astronomers a good view of a narrow section of the sky, indicated by shading here.

Mounting
The horseshoe shape of the mounting enables the telescope to tilt right up to the vertical, so that astronomers can look at the sky directly overhead.

Pressure bearings
The enormous telescope rests on oil pressure bearings: pumps force special oil into the bearings, so that the telescope floats on a bed of oil. This arrangement reduces friction so much that even a strong gust of wind can turn the 595-ton (540-tonne) weight of the telescope on its mounting.

Observer's cage
In most reflecting telescopes, the observer sees the image from the primary mirror by viewing its reflection in angled mirrors positioned inside the tube. However, the Hale telescope is so big that the astronomer can actually sit inside the tube. This position is called the prime (main) focus, because the primary mirror gathers light from the sky and focuses it (projects a clear image) here.

Radial knife edges
Girders called knife edges support the observer's cage, but are very thin so that they stop as little light as possible from reaching the primary mirror.

Telescope cage
To keep the mirrors the correct distance apart, the Hale telescope has steel beams arranged into a long, tube-shaped cage weighing 595 tons (540 tonnes). If the cage had been built to be completely rigid, it would have been impossibly heavy. So the cage is slightly flexible—but it is constructed so that the optical components remain in correct alignment even when the cage flexes slightly under its own weight.

Cool dome
The enclosed areas of the observatory are air conditioned.

Standard time equipment
Years ago, elaborate equipment was needed to measure time with the high degree of precision that astronomers demand. Today, computerized timekeeping equipment takes up much less space.

Equipment entrance
The observatory has an enormous door to provide access for heavy equipment.

Dome wall
The dome of the telescope weighs more than 1,102 tons (1,000 tonnes) and rests on wheeled trucks that run on rails around the edge of the observatory. Computer-controlled motors turn the dome to keep its opening aligned with the telescope.

Space pictures
The large darkroom dates from a time when astronomers used photographic plates to record their observations. Nowadays, most observations are made electronically.

Dial-a-star
Astronomers can dial in the position of any star they want to look at, and the telescope moves automatically into position.

Galleon

In the 16th century, large ships regularly set off across the blue Caribbean, carrying the plundered riches of the Americas back to Spain. With their billowing sails and creaking timbers, these galleons looked and sounded beautiful. But what would it have been like for the sailors? The first thing they would have noticed was the smell—a mixture of tar, bad drains, and sweat. With a daily water ration of little more than 1.2 gal (1 liter), there was not much left for washing. The ship was crowded and infested with fleas and rats. The food tasted disgusting, and most of the crew were constantly seasick. With a good wind, the journey from the Americas to Spain took more than 2 months. In calm conditions, or if a ship ran into rough weather, the journey could take even longer.

Place your bets
Many sailors gambled, betting on cards, dice, or almost anything that involved chance. Life on board a ship for months at a time was very dull, and the ship's crew welcomed any activity that filled the long hours off-duty.

Swivel guns
These small guns were nicknamed "murderers." They were used against enemy sailors.

Songs
Singing special songs called shanties helped the sailors work. The songs had a strong rhythm that helped the sailors to all heave at the same time.

It's about time
Everyone in the crew took turns at the watch (keeping look-out). Watches lasted 8 hours and were timed with an hourglass. Sand took half an hour to run through the narrow waist of this glass bottle.

Jardines
For lavatories, the crew used seats overhanging the deck rail. As a joke, they called them jardines—based on the French word for gardens.

Gratings
Structures called gratings let in light and air to the lower decks. They also let in lots of water.

Deck rail

Anchors aweigh!
The anchor cable ran around a huge drum called a capstan. The sailors turned the drum to weigh anchor (raise it).

Ram
The carved figure on the bow (front) of the ship could be used to ram enemy ships.

Soldiers
On Spanish fighting ships, the crew simply sailed the vessel and did not fight. Infantry (soldiers) operated the guns and attacked the enemy.

Stowaways
Thousands of rats lived on board the ship. In 1622, the sailors on one ship killed 4,000 rats during the voyage from the Caribbean to Europe. The rats that survived ate most of the ship's food.

Food storage
Ships carried olive oil for cooking in huge jars. Normally meat was pickled in salt water, but it was also preserved by hanging it from the deck rail in the salt spray. On one 17th-century voyage, sharks snapped at the meat dangling above the water!

Hull
The hull, or main body of the ship, was made entirely out of wood. It took hundreds of trees to build a really big wooden ship.

Sacks of food

An even keel
The keel was the backbone of the ship and helped it sail in a straight line. To stay upright, the ship carried ballast in the hold (storage area). Rocks and cannon balls made good ballast.

Water, water everywhere …
Everyone on board was allowed only 1.2 gal (1 liter) of water every day, or twice this amount of beer or cider. Every ship had to carry enough fresh water for the whole voyage, because sea water contains too much salt to drink.

Food and cooking
Each day, every member of the crew ate only 24½ oz (700 g) of biscuits and 8¾ oz (250 g) of dried meat or fish. Some days, they ate a dish of beans or peas as well. By the end of a long voyage, much of the food had gone bad, and the biscuits were filled with insects. When the sea was too rough, cooking was impossible, so the crew ate cheese instead of meat or fish.

KEY FACTS	
Typical length • about 141 ft (43 m)	
Keel length • 98 ft (30 m)	
Beam (width) • 36 ft (11 m)	
Weight • 551 tons (500 tonnes)	
Armament • 24 cannons firing 30-lb (14-kg) balls, 30 cannons firing 17½-lb (8-kg) balls, 2 swivel guns	

Heave-ho!
Everyone suffered from seasickness, even old sailors. Lemons were thought to be a cure, but were probably useless.

Please, God …
Spanish seamen say "He who goes to sea learns how to pray." A sea voyage could be terrifying, and people prayed that they would arrive safely.

Mainmast

Sew what
When sails became torn, the crew had to repair them by hand. Sails that were badly damaged were sometimes used for shrouds to wrap the bodies of sailors who died. Weighted with rocks, the body sank.

Livestock
Many ships carried pigs, sheep, and chickens. Fresh eggs and meat were reserved for the sick and the ship's most senior officers.

Sleeping
Sailors on the ship did not have cabins. They just slept wherever there was space.

What's that?
The crew looked at distant objects with a telescope, which made the objects appear bigger.

Large lantern

Decoration
The sterns (rear ends) of 17th-century sailing ships were painted in bright colors and had carved decoration. There were also big lanterns so other ships could see them at night.

Captain's cabin
The captain's cabin was the largest and most comfortable on the ship.

Treasure chests
Spanish ships returning from South America and the Caribbean often carried precious cargoes of gold. A strong chest kept the treasure safe during the voyage.

Lanterns
Strict regulations controlled the use of candles, because of the risk of fire.

Hinged gunport

At the helm
The helmsman steered the ship using a whipstaff—a long pole attached to the tiller. The tiller itself turned the rudder.

Big shots
Heavy carriage guns fired cannon balls (made of metal or stone), grapeshot (lumps of lead the size of grapes), or pieces of metal, which destroyed the rigging of enemy ships.

Whipstaff

Tiller

Barrels of gunpowder

Rudder

Close the gap
Ropes soaked in tar were used to seal the gaps between planks.

Spares
Damage to the rigging (the sails and ropes) was common, so every ship carried spares. Rats ate even the sails if they could, so spare sails were often stored in empty barrels.

Ballast

The galley
Cooking facilities were different on every ship. Often there was no chimney, so the kitchen (called a galley at sea) got very smoky.

A sting in the bale
Poisonous scorpions often lurked in the cargoes of wood that were carried in the hold.

A terrible smell
Sea water that seeped into the ship collected in the bilge—the space between the hold and the keel—and turned into a foul brew. This pump cleared the bilges, but the smell of the water was disgusting.

New horizons

In the 16th century, Spanish shipyards began to build a new kind of warship called a galleon. It was based on an earlier design called a carrack, but was narrower and more maneuverable. Naval guns had become powerful and accurate, and galleons were designed to use them effectively.

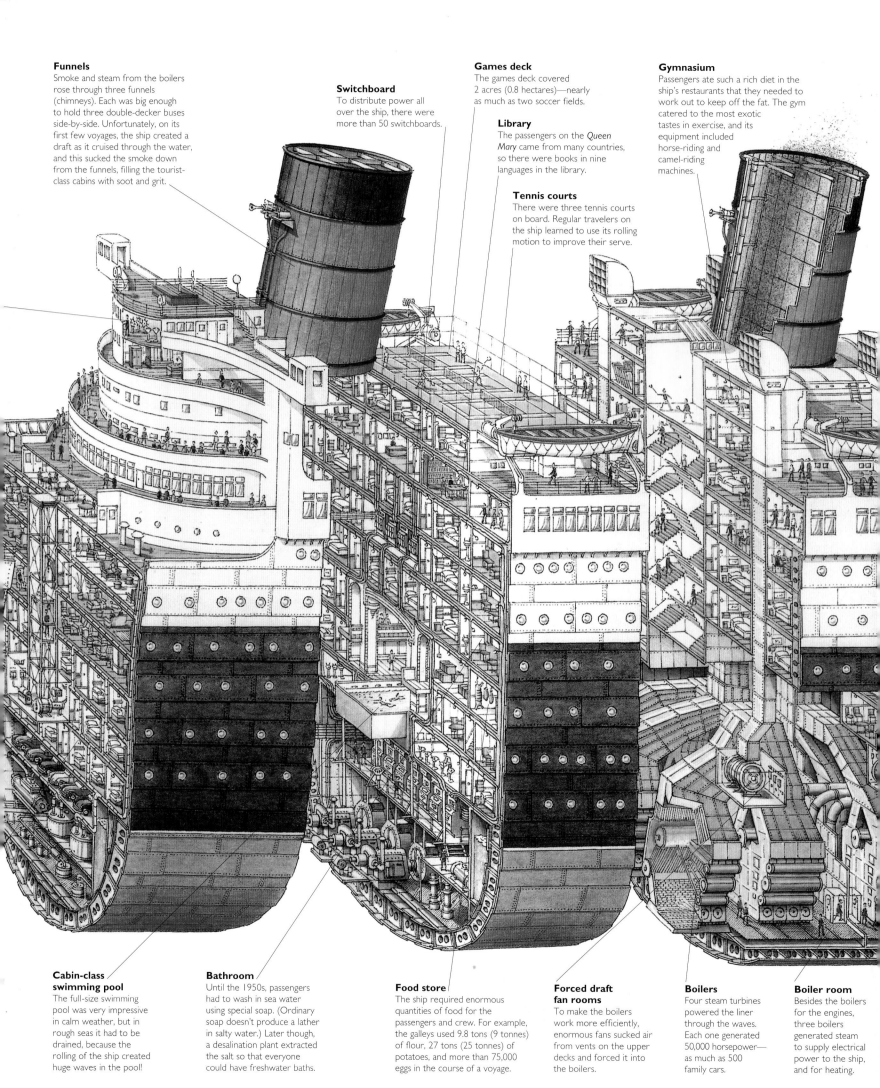

Funnels
Smoke and steam from the boilers rose through three funnels (chimneys). Each was big enough to hold three double-decker buses side-by-side. Unfortunately, on its first few voyages, the ship created a draft as it cruised through the water, and this sucked the smoke down from the funnels, filling the tourist-class cabins with soot and grit.

Switchboard
To distribute power all over the ship, there were more than 50 switchboards.

Games deck
The games deck covered 2 acres (0.8 hectares)—nearly as much as two soccer fields.

Library
The passengers on the *Queen Mary* came from many countries, so there were books in nine languages in the library.

Tennis courts
There were three tennis courts on board. Regular travelers on the ship learned to use its rolling motion to improve their serve.

Gymnasium
Passengers ate such a rich diet in the ship's restaurants that they needed to work out to keep off the fat. The gym catered to the most exotic tastes in exercise, and its equipment included horse-riding and camel-riding machines.

Cabin-class swimming pool
The full-size swimming pool was very impressive in calm weather, but in rough seas it had to be drained, because the rolling of the ship created huge waves in the pool!

Bathroom
Until the 1950s, passengers had to wash in sea water using special soap. (Ordinary soap doesn't produce a lather in salty water.) Later though, a desalination plant extracted the salt so that everyone could have freshwater baths.

Food store
The ship required enormous quantities of food for the passengers and crew. For example, the galleys used 9.8 tons (9 tonnes) of flour, 27 tons (25 tonnes) of potatoes, and more than 75,000 eggs in the course of a voyage.

Forced draft fan rooms
To make the boilers work more efficiently, enormous fans sucked air from vents on the upper decks and forced it into the boilers.

Boilers
Four steam turbines powered the liner through the waves. Each one generated 50,000 horsepower— as much as 500 family cars.

Boiler room
Besides the boilers for the engines, three boilers generated steam to supply electrical power to the ship, and for heating.

Ocean liner

When ocean travel was fast and fashionable, the world's great shipping lines battled for business just as airlines do today. In the 1930s, in a bid to be fastest across the Atlantic, Britain's Cunard Line built the *Queen Mary,* at that time the largest passenger liner in history. The prize for a fast liner was "The Blue Riband (ribbon) of the Atlantic," the honorary title given to the ship that made the fastest crossing between the United States and Europe. The *Queen Mary* won the Blue Riband in August 1936 by crossing the ocean in just under 4 days. A rival liner, the *Normandie,* regained the title the following year, but in August 1938, the *Queen Mary* took the title back, shaving 2 hours and 19 minutes off her previous record. The *Queen Mary* remained the fastest Atlantic passenger liner for 14 years and was used by film stars, politicians, and the rich and famous. The *Queen Mary* retired from passenger service in 1967 and is now permanently moored in California as a floating hotel and convention center.

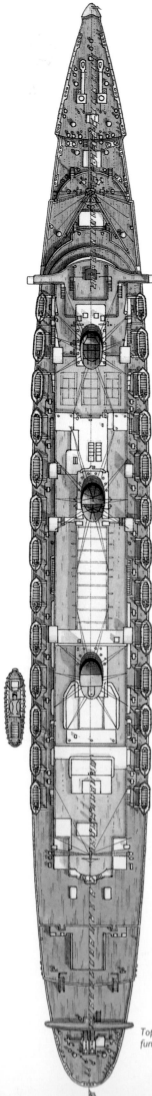

Top view showing funnels and decks

Side view showing superstructure

Length

The size of the *Queen Mary*—longer than six Statues of Liberty—created vast problems for both the ship's builders and for the New York port authorities. Before the ship could be built, an enormous dry-dock had to be constructed in Britain. In New York, a special 1,000-ft (305-m) pier was built.

LENGTH IN METERS

0	15	30	45	60	75	90	105	120	135	150

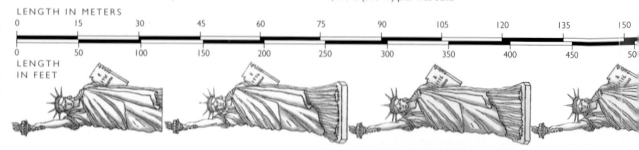

0	50	100	150	200	250	300	350	400	450	50

LENGTH IN FEET

Gull's-eye view

Seen from above, the tiny tennis courts give a sense of the enormous scale of the *Queen Mary*'s decks. Rigged in constant readiness, the lifeboats were capable of carrying 145 people each. Fortunately, they never had to be used.

The route

The *Queen Mary* sailed between New York and Southampton, on Britain's south coast. The liner's owners built the ship to run a weekly service between the two ports. To make the crossing in less than 5 days and beat the record of other shipping lines, the *Queen Mary* had to average 28.5 knots (33 mph / 53 kph).

New York

Ocean liner

Crossing the Atlantic Ocean today in a supersonic airliner requires just a few hours of considerable discomfort, but in 1936, things were different. Traveling between Britain and New York meant a sea voyage lasting at least 4 days—only the most daring flew. Shipping companies of the time competed to provide their passengers with the fastest, most luxurious crossing. It was this competition that led to the construction of the *Queen Mary*. When this enormous ship was built, she was the fastest passenger liner in the world, and probably the most luxurious. The ship's owners, the Cunard Line, spent millions to create a vast floating hotel as good as any found on land.

The *Queen Mary* had three classes of passengers, just like the First, Business, and Coach classes on an airliner. Cabin-class passengers had suites of rooms with fresh flowers and adjoining cabins for their servants. Tourist-class passengers had less fancy rooms, but they still traveled in some style. Third-class passengers paid the least for their tickets, and they got plain cabins in the noisiest, smokiest part of the ship. However, the Atlantic wind and waves did not know or care how much each passenger had paid for a ticket. Those in Cabin and Third class suffered equally from seasickness. And how they suffered! Nobody had built a ship as big as the *Queen Mary* before, and her designers had no idea how the Atlantic waves would toss and roll the ship. In the worst seas, the *Queen Mary* rolled 44 degrees.

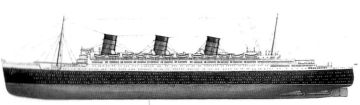

Naming a Queen

There are many stories about the *Queen Mary*, some true and some untrue. One of the untrue stories is that Cunard originally wanted to name their new liner the *Queen Victoria*. When the company approached King George V for his permission, they said that the new ship was to be named after the greatest queen in English history. The King said that his wife would be delighted. His wife, of course, was Queen Mary.

Everything that was not attached to the floor moved around. In one of the larger rooms, a piano broke free of its attachments, and crashed from side to side. It smashed against the costly furniture and paneling, emitting eerie twangs.

The ship's owners acted quickly. With the aid of carefully positioned ballast (balancing weights), they made sure that the *Queen Mary* cut more smoothly through the waves. Soon the world's rich and famous lined up to buy tickets.

Salons and beauty parlors
These offered every service that you might expect in a beauty salon on land, including Swedish massages and mudpacks. If you were curious, you could even have an x-ray. (This was before the harmful effects of x-rays were realized.)

Earplugs supplied
There were many musicians on board to entertain the passengers. So that they could practice without disturbing other passengers, there was a soundproofed studio with a piano.

Elevator
There was a total of 21 elevators on board. They weren't just a luxury, because the ship was as tall as a 12-story building. Moving supplies from deck to deck would have been very difficult without elevators.

Kennels
Dogs were luxuriously accommodated in 26 kennels. They even had their own 78¾-ft (24-m) exercise area—and a lamppost.

Carpets
There were 6 miles (9.6 km) of carpets on board, all of them specially woven for the *Queen Mary*.

Bridge
High above the front decks was the bridge. From here, the captain controlled the ship, and officers were on duty 24 hours a day to keep the ship on course. They also kept a lookout for icebergs—a frequent hazard in the North Atlantic.

Flowers
Hundreds of bunches of fresh flowers beautified the ship. They were all changed at the end of each trip. The *Queen Mary* had four gardeners.

Fuel
The ship used an average of 1,102 tons (1,000 tonnes) of fuel a day.

Keel
The keel of the *Queen Mary* was made of huge plates 29½ ft (9 m) long and 6 ft (1.8 m) deep, joined by riveted straps. The hull was plated with steel plates about 1 in (2.5 cm) thick and was either double- or triple-riveted.

Lighting
The 30,000 light bulbs on the ship required constant attention. A team of electricians spent half the night changing blown bulbs while the passengers were asleep.

Prow and props

The *Queen Mary*'s white superstructure and red funnels made an awe-inspiring sight. 18,000 scale model tests ensured that the ship's towering bow (front) would cut cleanly through the water, powered forward by four 19½-ft (6-m) diameter propellers 984¼ ft (300 m) to the rear at the stern (back) of the ship.

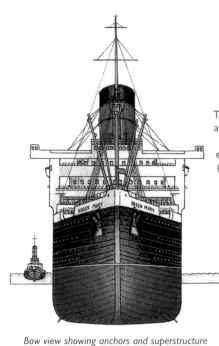

Bow view showing anchors and superstructure

Stern view showing rudder and propellers

Decks and cabins

Careful planning enforced a strict social class system on board the ship. The height above the waterline indicated status: passengers who paid the most for their tickets had airy views from the upper decks.

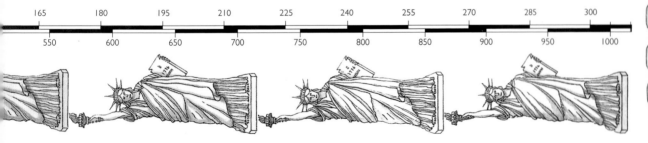

165	180	195	210	225	240	255	270	285	300
550	600	650	700	750	800	850	900	950	1000

Cunard

The Cunard Line was founded in 1839 by Samuel (later Sir Samuel) Cunard. Cunard started a transatlantic passenger service between Britain and the United States. Cunard's first ship was the *Britannia*, on which British author Charles Dickens traveled to New York in 1842.

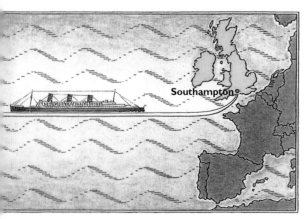

Southampton

The hull

Ten million rivets held together the 160 watertight compartments that divided up the vast hull. If the ship was holed, the water would fill only one compartment, and the ship would not sink. At the stern (rear) of the ship was the rudder, which was as big as a house and weighed 198 tons (180 tonnes).

Bottom view showing propellers and keel

Coal mine

Inside a low tunnel 1,640 ft (500 m) underground, coal miners operate machines that take great bites out of Earth's crust to extract coal from rock. This coal will then be used in power stations, where it is burned to produce the electricity that lights many people's homes and powers their machines and devices.

People have been burning coal for thousands of years. At first, they probably used coal that they found on the surface of the ground. However, they soon began to dig pits and shafts to find coal seams—layers of coal buried in the rocks underground. In these early mines, miners risked their lives daily to dig out the "black gold" using pickaxes and shovels. This coal mine is shown operating in the 1990s. Today's miners are helped by computers and giant diggers, but mines are still dark, damp, dirty, and dangerous places.

Mining machinery

The modern mine relies on machinery, not muscle power, to extract coal. The vicious-looking **road heading machine** uses its spinning bit to drill out the roads to the coal face (the part of the mine where coal is actually being dug out). The **shearer loader** moves across the coal face, tearing through coal and rock with diamond-tipped blades attached to a rotating drum. **Powered roof supports** hold up the roof as the shearer loader advances. The supports also push the conveyor, which carries coal away from the face.

Road heading machine

Shearer loader

Powered roof supports

Pit head
Most of the mine is below ground, but work also takes place on the surface. The offices and workshops above ground are called the pit head.

Back to nature
A vast amount of work is being undertaken to restore the sites of old collieries and return them to nature.

Landscaping
In the past, mining was not attractive, but modern pits have been designed to blend in with the landscape to minimize the impact on surroundings.

Finding coal
Coal is found underground in thin layers called seams. Some coal seams are up to 19¾ ft (6 m) thick, but seams as thin as 78¾ in (200 cm) may still contain enough coal to be worthwhile mining.

Moving coal
Coal is rarely mined where it is needed, so trains and heavy carts carry it away from the mine.

Showers
At the pit head, the miners can have showers and a meal. Everyone has a locker to store their working clothes when they go home.

Canteen

Bright idea
To see in the darkness of the pit, every miner has a battery-powered lamp. The lamp is strapped to a helmet so that the miner's hands are free. The miners recharge the batteries of their lamps in the lamp room.

Sorting shafts

Cleaning and grading
Coal that comes out of the mine is mixed with a lot of mud and rock. Before the lumps of coal can be sold, they must be cleaned and graded—sorted into different qualities and sizes. Tanks of water separate coal from rock: the coal floats, but the rock sinks.

Tunnel supports

Winding gear
Powerful winches at the top of the shaft raise skips of coal to the surface and lower miners down the shaft in a cage—a kind of elevator.

Store
In the pithead buildings, there are stores and workshops where apparatus needed in the mine can be assembled.

Recreation hall

Parking lot

Ventilation shaft

Fan housing

Fan house
Huge fans suck stale air out of the mine and draw fresh air in.

Moving underground
Mines use many different sorts of transportation. In the larger roads, electric or diesel locomotives haul trains. Free Steered Vehicles (FSVs) are diesel-powered tractor units that also move miners and equipment.

Fan blades

Upcast shaft
Every mine has at least two shafts. Stale air is drawn out of the mine through the upcast shaft.

Conveyor

Coal separators

Elevator to transport miners to coal face

Coal seam

Trunk road
The main tunnels of the mine are called trunk roads, just like the roads linking cities on the surface.

Ventilation door
Doors control the flow of fresh air around the mine. Opening a sliding panel in the door increases the flow of air. Doors are in sets of three, so that there are always two doors shut, and air cannot escape.

Air crossing
The flow of air through the roads of the mine is very important, and where roads cross, they sometimes snake over each other so that fresh and stale air do not mix.

All aboard!
The coal face may be many miles away from the shaft. Miners travel by train to where they are working.

Skip
To winch coal to the surface, it is loaded into a skip—a huge steel box holding 11 tons (10 tonnes). In drift mines, skips are not used. Instead, the coal travels to the surface on a conveyor, up a drift—a long sloping tunnel.

Bunker
Coal waiting to be loaded is stored temporarily in underground bunkers that hold up to 60 skip loads. Other bunkers, designed to hold coal underground in case of a conveyor breakdown, have a much larger capacity of up to 1,102 tons (1,000 tonnes).

Vertical track for elevator

Fresh air
Ventilation allows the miners to breathe and keeps the working areas from getting too hot. Also, without good ventilation, methane—an explosive gas—would collect in the tunnels. In the past, mine explosions were a common occurrence.

Walking to work
Trains cannot reach every part of the mine, so miners walk some of the way to where they are working.

Downcast shaft
Fresh air flows into the mine down the downcast shaft to replace the stale air sucked out by the fans in the upcast shaft.

Water jets
Dust is a constant hazard: clouds of it can explode, and miners in the past suffered from diseases as a result of inhaling dust. To keep dust down, water jets spray the coal whenever it is cut or moved around.

Coal on wheels
The area where coal is extracted from the seam is called the coal face. Tubs pulled by a locomotive take some of the coal from the face to the skips, which will raise it to the surface.

Gate roads
A road heading machine cuts the two gate roads at either end of the coal face. Coal seams are rarely level, so the road heading machine often has to climb steep hills underground.

Coal face

A real support
Steel plates support the roof where coal has been cut away.

Shear power
At the heart of the coal mine is the shearer loader. As it cuts coal from the face, the shearer loader moves slowly back and forth between the two gate roads, advancing the face about 27½ in (70 cm) at each pass.

Armored flexible conveyor
From the shearer loader, coal drops onto the armored flexible conveyor (AFC). This is an endless belt of coupled steel sections, which are kept moving by a motor.

Gate belt conveyor
Coal from the AFC is loaded onto a gate belt conveyor that moves it along the gate road to the nearest trunk road.

Trunk conveyor
Coal from the gate belt conveyor drops onto a trunk conveyor. This carries it along the trunk road to a shaft.

Tank

Five centuries ago, the Italian artist and inventor Leonardo da Vinci (1452–1519) dreamed up terrible fighting machines. They could cross muddy battlefields with ease, and metal armor protected them from attack. By the start of World War II in 1939, European armies were equipped with large numbers of tanks, all formidable fighting machines, equipped with linked steel caterpillar tracks so that they could cross any terrain in any weather.

Fighting in a tank such as the Soviet T-34 shown here was a horrible job. The inside of the tank was incredibly cramped, noisy, and uncomfortable. Ammunition and fuel enclosed the crew on all sides, so a direct hit from an enemy shell usually made the tank explode or catch fire. Despite the danger, tanks proved to be very successful.

Big shot
The tank's gun was a formidable weapon. It could fire high-explosive, armor-piercing, or shrapnel shells. The armor-piercing shells could penetrate 2½ in (65 mm) of armor plating.

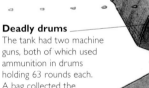

Rifling
Grooves in the barrel made the shells spin and follow a straight path.

What did you say?
Until 1943, few tanks had radios. Crews had to use signal flags to send messages to other tanks.

Deadly drums
The tank had two machine guns, both of which used ammunition in drums holding 63 rounds each. A bag collected the spent cartridge cases.

Air cylinders
The tank had an electric starter motor, but if this failed, the crew could start the engine using compressed air from cylinders at the front of the tank.

Accelerator

Driver
The driver controlled the tank using two steering levers, each of which started or stopped one of the two tracks to turn the tank.

Brake

Clutch

Elevation control
Turning the elevation wheel raised or lowered the gun. The control was hard to operate, and if the gunner had long legs, the wheel banged his knees when he turned it.

Dual role
This tank had a crew of only four (most tanks have crews of five or more) so the commander also had to act as gunner. In practice he was overworked and did neither job well.

In its sights
The gunner/commander aimed the gun using one of two sights. One provided a view through a periscope on the turret roof. The other gun-sight was a telescope pointing directly forward.

Loader
The loader had an uncomfortable job. The ammunition bin lids were hard to get off, and the cramped turret made it difficult to lift the 21-lb (9.5-kg) shells to the breech of the gun.

Hinge

Wireless aerial

KEY FACTS

Length • 20 ft (6.08 m)	
Width • 10 ft (3 m)	
Weight • 31 tons (28.25 tonnes)	
Top speed • 31 mph (50 kph) approx	
Engine power • 500 horsepower	
Gearbox • Four speeds forward, one reverse	

Foot firing
The gunner/commander used pedals to fire the main gun and one of the machine guns. The loader could also fire both guns with hand triggers.

Shell collection
Shells were hard to reach. They were mainly stored in bins under the gunner's feet. In battle, the turret quickly became strewn with open ammunition bins.

Guide-horn
A guide-horn on alternate links kept the links engaged with the tank's wheels.

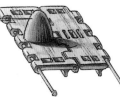

Design flaw
The turret hatch opened forward, but when open, it blocked the view of the way ahead. Consequently, Soviet tank commanders could not observe the battle from the open hatch without exposing themselves to enemy fire.

Tough turret
The T-34's turret housed the large gun and could rotate around. It was made of very hard steel armor plate.

Electric traverse motor

Crude construction
T-34 tanks were crudely made compared to their German and British counterparts. Soviet engineering was primitive and resources scarce, so the factories carefully ground and polished only where absolutely necessary. However, the rough finish did not reduce the tank's effectiveness.

All the way around
There was a motor to traverse, or rotate, the turret, and the gunner could also use a hand-wheel for traversing. However, the hand-wheel was in an awkward position, and the gunner had to reach across and turn it with his right hand.

Narrow view
The gunner/commander could see the battlefield through a periscope, but this provided a very narrow field of view.

Last resort
If the tank crew ran out of shells and ammunition for their machine guns, they defended themselves by firing handguns through these tiny ports.

Turret seats
The turret crew sat on seats attached to the turret itself. When the turret turned, they turned with it.

Fuel tank

Plenty of power
The tank's 10-gal (39-liter) V-12 engine generated 500 horsepower. It was capable of propelling the tank at speeds of up to 31 mph (50 kph) on a good road.

Engine air filter

Engine covering

Engine cooling fane

Exhaust pipe

Deadly weapon

When the Soviet T-34 tank first appeared in 1941, it was without doubt the best-designed tank in the world. It was highly mobile, had a powerful gun, and had very solid armor. Unfortunately, the tanks were manufactured in a great hurry, so some parts were crudely made and of poor quality. In addition, Soviet tank crews often only received 72 hours of training before going into action.

What, no bathroom?
You'll notice that there are no "facilities" on board the tank. The crew either left the tank or used an empty shell case to answer the call of nature.

Gearbox
The tank's gearbox was very easy to reach for maintenance. This was fortunate, since early models had serious defects. Gearbox problems immobilized more tanks in 1941 than enemy action.

Amazing armor
The high quality of the T-34 armor plating meant that the tank could withstand attack better than the German Pz Kpfw III tanks that it met in battle. The armor was 1¾ in (45 mm) thick on the turret front, but in later models, this was increased to 2½ in (65 mm).

Towing cables

Gripping grousers
Bolt-on plates, called grousers, provided extra grip in mud or snow.

Wheels
Owing to a shortage of rubber in 1942, T-34 tanks began to be made with solid metal wheels. However, this caused terrible vibration, which shook parts loose. The problem was solved by putting rubber treads on the first and fifth wheels.

Suspension
The tank's suspension gave a comfortable ride but made it difficult to aim the gun accurately while the tank was moving. Modern tanks solve this problem by using devices to stabilize the gun.

Making tracks
The manganese steel tracks spread the enormous weight of the tank so that it did not sink into the mud of the battlefield. Ground pressure beneath the track was very low—only about double the pressure under a human foot.

Oil rig

Filling a car's fuel tank is easy, but extracting oil from which to make the fuel is extremely difficult. To understand the challenge of drilling for oil, think about standing at the top of a 6½-ft (2-m) step ladder. Most of the ladder is underwater. Now drill a hole the width of a pencil in the ground beneath the ladder. You need a very long drill, because the hole is 98 ft (30 m) deep. Sounds difficult? Drilling for oil at sea is much harder.

Much of the world's oil is buried under the sea. Giant oil production platforms may be more than 705 ft (215 m) high, but only a quarter shows above the waves. The rest is a strong frame anchored to the sea bed. The platform supports the rig—the apparatus that drills down to the oil, as well as storage tanks, pumps, and living quarters for the workers, who live on the rig for 2 weeks at a time.

Around the clock
Kitchens on the rig stay open day and night. Oil production is continuous, and there are people working all the time.

Loading bay
A crane unloads supplies from a small ship when the weather is calm enough for the ship to safely sail close to the platform.

Accommodation block
More than 100 workers live on the rig. It is home for 2 weeks at a time, so everything they need for work and recreation is supplied.

Helicopter landing pad
Workers and supplies arrive by helicopter. In very bad weather, ships cannot reach the platform, and the helicopter is the only link to the mainland.

Control room
All the operations of the platform can be monitored and managed from here. Computers help control the flow of gas and oil.

Gas
Most wells produce gas as well as oil. Gas is used in the platform's power plant.

Movie theater
Boredom is a big problem for offshore workers, but a movie theater breaks up the monotony.

Power station
The platform uses electricity for powering systems such as heating and lighting and also for pumping gas and oil ashore.

Drilling for Oil

The part of the platform that drills down to reach the oil reserves is called the rig. The rig's motor turns a rotary table, which then turns a long shaft, called the drill string, which has a drill bit on the end. The drill bit has hard teeth which cut through the rock below. As the shaft gets deeper, the drillers add on 29-ft (9-m) long pieces of pipe. The most visible part of the entire oil platform, called the derrick, is 196 ft (60 m) high and supports the winch and crane, which hold up the drill string. The drill string may weigh hundreds of tons, and the crane must be powerful enough to pull the entire string from the shaft.

As drilling progresses, a mix of chemicals called mud is pumped down the drill string to keep the drill bit cool and bring rocks to the surface. The mud pipe then carries the mud back to the platform. The mud is filtered and pumped back down the drill string.

When a drill strikes oil, the shaft becomes a producing well. An arrangement of valves called a Christmas tree is fitted to the top of the shaft and regulates the flow of oil from the well. A single production platform may have as many as 30–40 wells.

If a drill bit strikes oil or gas under pressure, there can be a blow-out—oil or gas rushes up the drill pipe and gushes out. A device called a blow-out preventer guards against this.

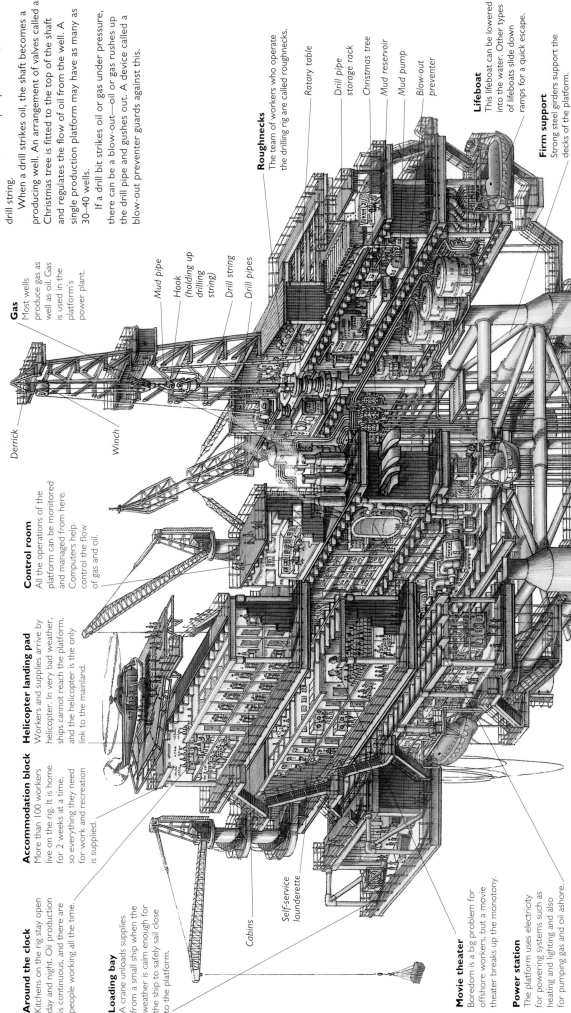

Derrick

Winch

Mud pipe

Hook (holding up drilling string)

Drill string

Drill pipes

Roughnecks
The team of workers who operate the drilling rig are called roughnecks.

Rotary table

Drill pipe storage rack

Christmas tree

Mud reservoir

Mud pump

Blow-out preventer

Lifeboat
This lifeboat can be lowered into the water. Other types of lifeboats slide down ramps for a quick escape.

Firm support
Strong steel girders support the decks of the platform.

Cabins

Self-service launderette

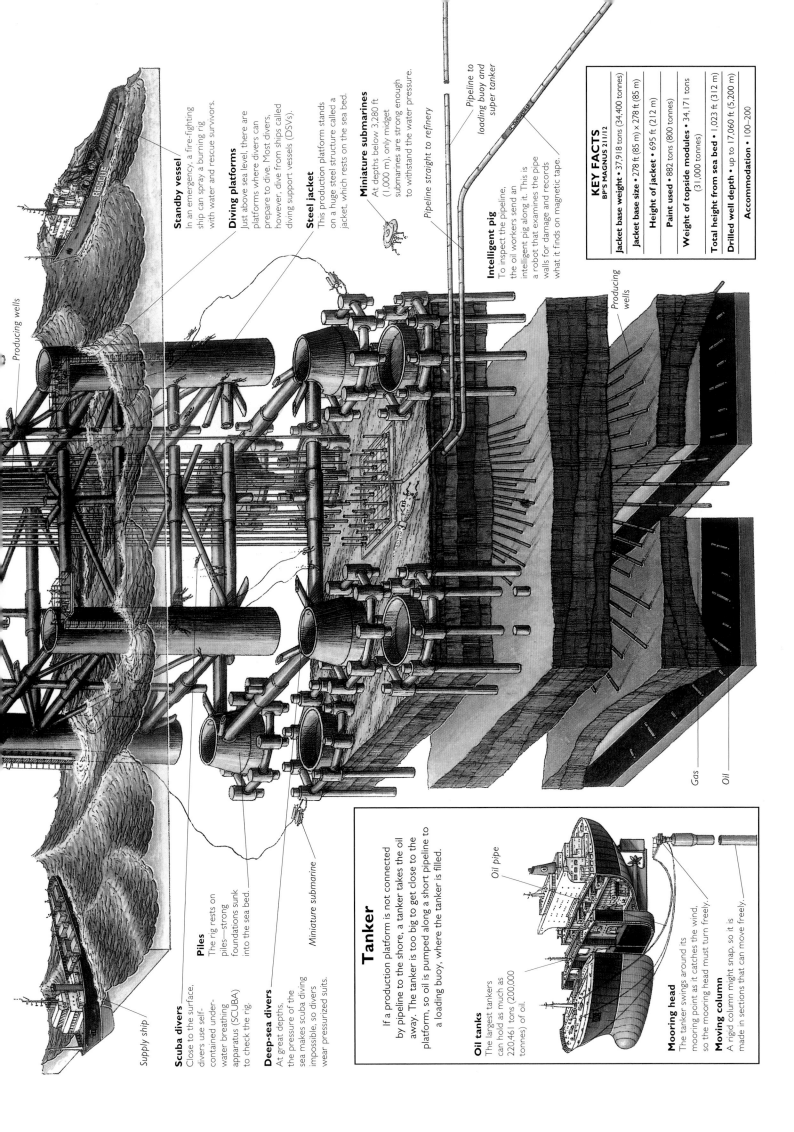

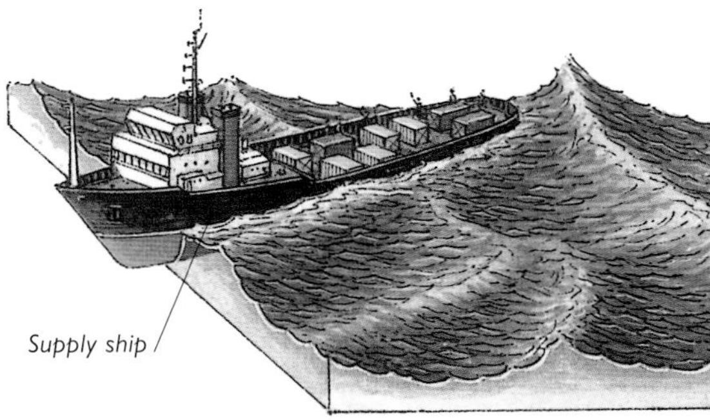
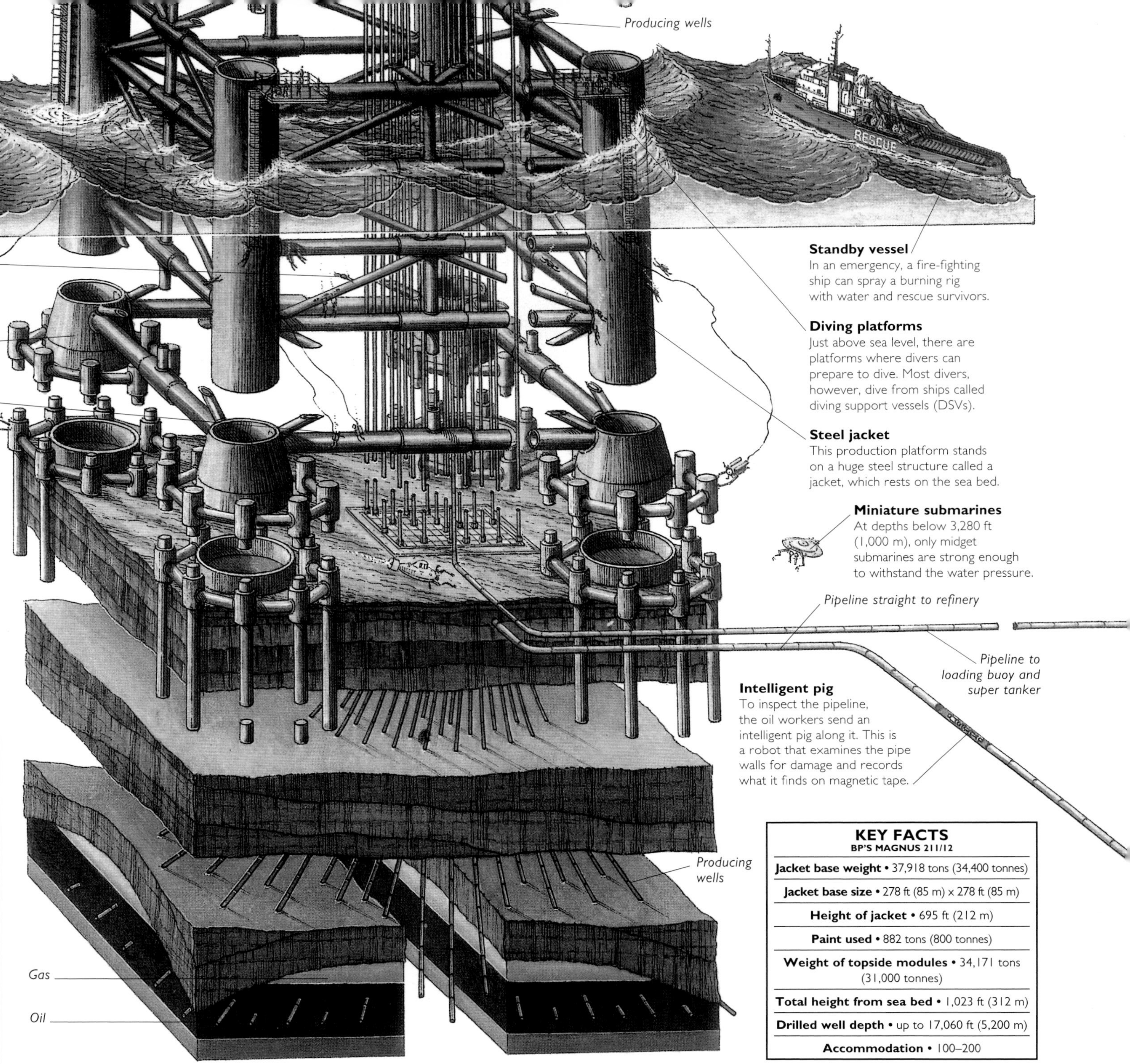
Producing wells
Supply ship
RESCUE
Miniature submarine
Pipeline straight to refinery
Pipeline to loading buoy and super tanker
Producing wells
Gas
Oil

Scuba divers
Close to the surface, divers use self-contained under-water breathing apparatus (SCUBA) to check the rig.

Piles
The rig rests on piles—strong foundations sunk into the sea bed.

Deep-sea divers
At great depths, the pressure of the sea makes scuba diving impossible, so divers wear pressurized suits.

Standby vessel
In an emergency, a fire-fighting ship can spray a burning rig with water and rescue survivors.

Diving platforms
Just above sea level, there are platforms where divers can prepare to dive. Most divers, however, dive from ships called diving support vessels (DSVs).

Steel jacket
This production platform stands on a huge steel structure called a jacket, which rests on the sea bed.

Miniature submarines
At depths below 3,280 ft (1,000 m), only midget submarines are strong enough to withstand the water pressure.

Intelligent pig
To inspect the pipeline, the oil workers send an intelligent pig along it. This is a robot that examines the pipe walls for damage and records what it finds on magnetic tape.

Tanker

If a production platform is not connected by pipeline to the shore, a tanker takes the oil away. The tanker is too big to get close to the platform, so oil is pumped along a short pipeline to a loading buoy, where the tanker is filled.

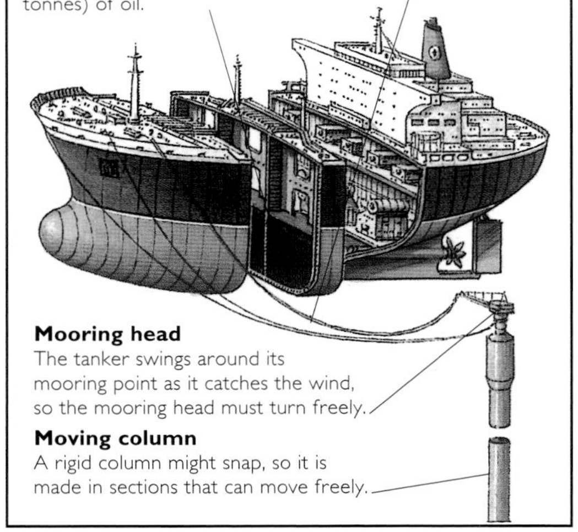
Oil pipe

Oil tanks
The largest tankers can hold as much as 220,461 tons (200,000 tonnes) of oil.

Mooring head
The tanker swings around its mooring point as it catches the wind, so the mooring head must turn freely.

Moving column
A rigid column might snap, so it is made in sections that can move freely.

KEY FACTS
BP'S MAGNUS 211/12

Jacket base weight • 37,918 tons (34,400 tonnes)
Jacket base size • 278 ft (85 m) x 278 ft (85 m)
Height of jacket • 695 ft (212 m)
Paint used • 882 tons (800 tonnes)
Weight of topside modules • 34,171 tons (31,000 tonnes)
Total height from sea bed • 1,023 ft (312 m)
Drilled well depth • up to 17,060 ft (5,200 m)
Accommodation • 100–200

Cathedral

Soaring high over the city skyline, the spires and roofs of a cathedral are a breathtaking sight. Cathedrals are just as amazing inside. They astonish the visitor with stained glass and with beautiful stone and wood carved into intricate shapes and patterns. Creating a cathedral today would be an enormous and expensive task. And when most European cathedrals were built centuries ago, everything in them had to be laboriously carved by hand. Cathedral builders were not thinking about modern tourists when they began their work. They were building a place of prayer and worship, for the glory of God.

Today, cathedrals still play an important part in the Christian religion. Each is the special central church of a diocese (religious district). The bishop of the diocese leads the worship in the cathedral.

Jewel of France

The cathedral cross-section on these pages is based on the famous cathedral at Chartres, France. This was built between the years 1195–1260 and is considered by many experts to be the most perfect of Europe's cathedrals. The original builders of Chartres envisioned the completed structure with nine towers, but only two were completed.

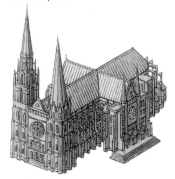

This is a view of the cathedral as it stands today.

The original plan of the cathedral had nine towers, including a massive central spire.

Niches
On the front of the cathedral, there are many statues, each in a niche (an individual alcove). Today, most of the statues are just plain stone-colored, but they were once painted in bright hues.

Main entrance
Most people enter the cathedral through a door in the west front.

Buttress

Nave
The people who come to worship in the cathedral enter the nave, the main body of the cathedral. Today, there are usually pews (seats) here, but for many centuries, the nave was an open area where worshippers stood.

Staircase
Climbing a lot of stairs is the only way to reach the roof, and this partly explains why fire destroyed so many cathedrals. To put out the flames, people passed buckets of water from hand to hand. Much of the water sloshed out by the time the buckets reached the fire.

Bells
Bells were installed in the tower of the cathedral to call people to worship. The biggest often weighed more than 1.1 tons (1 tonne). A group of bells with different notes is called a peal. They can be rung in thousands of different combinations.

Spitting water
Rainwater spouted from the roof through the mouths of grotesque stone figures called gargoyles.

Flying buttresses
The cathedral's builders used buttresses to support the weight of the roof. These are great stone columns built on the outside of the cathedral. They carry the weight down to the ground. Flying buttresses have arches that hold up the upper parts of the walls.

Triforium
Halfway up the wall of the cathedral is the triforium: an arched passageway.

Maze
Many cathedrals of the Middle Ages (c. 500–1450) had mazes built into the floors. A walk along the maze probably represented a pilgrimage (holy journey) to the ancient city of Jerusalem in the Holy Land.

Crypt
Underneath much of the cathedral is a crypt—a kind of cellar. Often, the crypt is a burial place for officials of the church and other important people.

Meet the team

Bishop

Priests & Canons

Pilgrim

Master mason

Cutter *Plumber* *Sawyer* *Carpenter*

Woodman *Setter* *Glazier* *Smith* *Laborer*

The **bishop** was the leader of worship in the cathedral. He had help in organizing worship from **priests** and **canons**, and possibly from monks if the cathedral was attached to a monastery.

The **master mason**, who designed the structure, led the building team. **Cutters** shaped the stone and **setters** put it in place. **Sawyers** cut timber and **carpenters** made all the wooden parts of the cathedral, including the scaffolding the others worked from. **Smiths** made the metal fittings and **glaziers** the beautiful windows.

Organ
Music has been important in Christian worship for centuries. Organs were first used in European cathedrals more than a thousand years ago.

Roof beams
The cathedral roof is a network of huge timbers and thin strips of wood. A thin skin of lead or copper makes the roof waterproof.

Stained glass
Stained-glass windows held thousands of pieces of colored glass. Each window told a Bible story in pictures.

Brick vaulting (curved ceilings)

Choir
The part of the cathedral where the choir stand to sing is also called the choir. The choir and altar were separated from the rest of the church by a partition called a rood screen.

Presbytery
The bishop and priests traditionally lead worship in the cathedral from the presbytery, an area at the eastern end containing the altar.

Altar
The altar itself is the most important place in the cathedral. Some may have been placed according to where the sun rose on the saint's day of the cathedral. For instance, St. Patrick's day is on March 17, so in a cathedral dedicated to (named for) St. Patrick, the altar was aligned with the sunrise on March 17.

Shaping the arches
To make sure that all the pieces of stone fitted together, the masons used templates. These were wooden patterns made full size. As they carved the stone, the masons held the templates against the stonework to make sure they didn't chip too much away.

Apse
The eastern end of the cathedral, called the apse, is often semicircular in shape. The altar is at the center of the apse.

Lady chapel
Many cathedrals have chapels dedicated to the Virgin Mary, Jesus Christ's mother. The chapel is called the "Lady Chapel" because Mary is also called "Our Lady."

Ambulatory
Surrounding the apse is an ambulatory, or walkway.

Chantry chapel
Wealthy supporters of the cathedral often gave money to have a chapel built in their memory when they died. They also paid for a priest to say Mass there, because they thought that this would help them get into heaven.

Solid foundations
Every cathedral needed lots of stone in its construction. Strong foundations supported the huge weight of the building above.

Chip off the old block
Much of the cathedral was prefabricated: masons carved the stonework roughly to shape at the quarry and finished it off on the building site.

Transept
The transepts cross the nave. They make the plan of the cathedral into a cross shape, to remind Christians of the wooden cross on which Christ was nailed.

Throngs of people
Enormous numbers of tourists visit Europe's great cathedrals to wonder at the beautiful craftsmanship. Some pause and pray. In the past, cathedrals were just as crowded, but with pilgrims—people who traveled to cathedrals for prayer and worship.

Shrine
Cathedrals often had shrines. These were chambers containing relics—objects of special religious importance, such as the bones of a saint or a piece of Christ's cross. Many people visited cathedrals to worship at shrines.

Jumbo jet

Imagine a small town and all its people flying through the air at hundreds of miles an hour. Imagine this flying town has power, heating, and sewage plants and carries enough food and drink to keep everyone well-fed. Now imagine hundreds of such towns flying high above tall mountains, deep oceans, and polar icecaps. They carry their human cargo to a strict timetable, in greater

safety than a car. But this flying town is not imaginary. It is a Boeing 747 airplane, or jumbo jet, and it can carry more than 400 people. When the 747 began service in 1969, it was the world's largest passenger airplane and would remain so until 2007. The aircraft shown here was one of the first—Pan Am's N732.

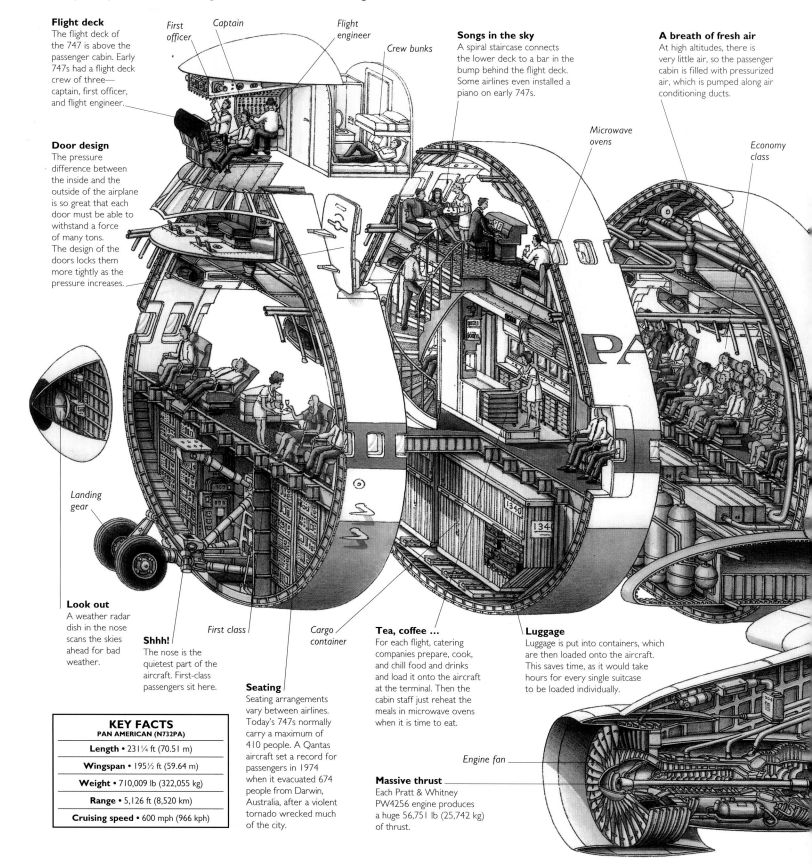

Flight deck
The flight deck of the 747 is above the passenger cabin. Early 747s had a flight deck crew of three— captain, first officer, and flight engineer.

First officer

Captain

Flight engineer

Crew bunks

Door design
The pressure difference between the inside and the outside of the airplane is so great that each door must be able to withstand a force of many tons. The design of the doors locks them more tightly as the pressure increases.

Songs in the sky
A spiral staircase connects the lower deck to a bar in the bump behind the flight deck. Some airlines even installed a piano on early 747s.

A breath of fresh air
At high altitudes, there is very little air, so the passenger cabin is filled with pressurized air, which is pumped along air conditioning ducts.

Microwave ovens

Economy class

Landing gear

Look out
A weather radar dish in the nose scans the skies ahead for bad weather.

Shhh!
The nose is the quietest part of the aircraft. First-class passengers sit here.

First class

Cargo container

Tea, coffee ...
For each flight, catering companies prepare, cook, and chill food and drinks and load it onto the aircraft at the terminal. Then the cabin staff just reheat the meals in microwave ovens when it is time to eat.

Luggage
Luggage is put into containers, which are then loaded onto the aircraft. This saves time, as it would take hours for every single suitcase to be loaded individually.

Seating
Seating arrangements vary between airlines. Today's 747s normally carry a maximum of 410 people. A Qantas aircraft set a record for passengers in 1974 when it evacuated 674 people from Darwin, Australia, after a violent tornado wrecked much of the city.

Engine fan

Massive thrust
Each Pratt & Whitney PW4256 engine produces a huge 56,751 lb (25,742 kg) of thrust.

KEY FACTS	
PAN AMERICAN (N732PA)	
Length • 231¼ ft (70.51 m)	
Wingspan • 195½ ft (59.64 m)	
Weight • 710,009 lb (322,055 kg)	
Range • 5,126 ft (8,520 km)	
Cruising speed • 600 mph (966 kph)	

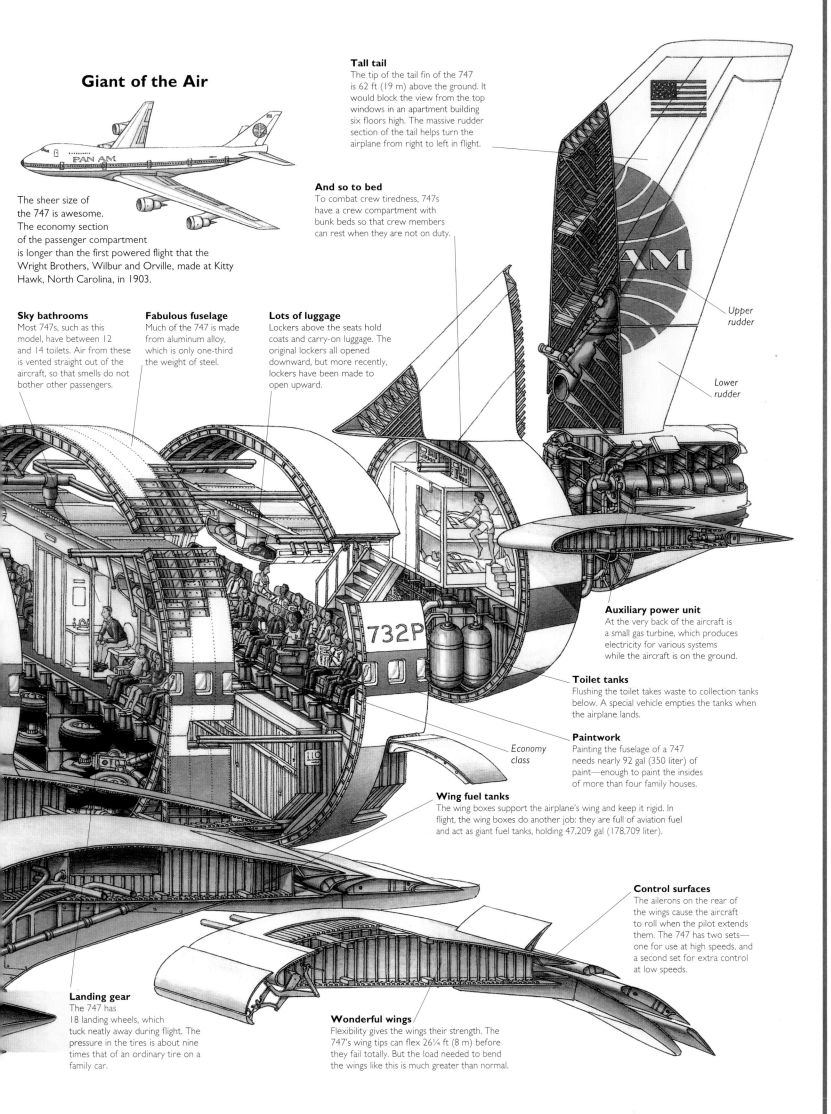

Giant of the Air

The sheer size of
the 747 is awesome.
The economy section
of the passenger compartment
is longer than the first powered flight that the
Wright Brothers, Wilbur and Orville, made at Kitty
Hawk, North Carolina, in 1903.

Tall tail
The tip of the tail fin of the 747
is 62 ft (19 m) above the ground. It
would block the view from the top
windows in an apartment building
six floors high. The massive rudder
section of the tail helps turn the
airplane from right to left in flight.

And so to bed
To combat crew tiredness, 747s
have a crew compartment with
bunk beds so that crew members
can rest when they are not on duty.

Sky bathrooms
Most 747s, such as this
model, have between 12
and 14 toilets. Air from these
is vented straight out of the
aircraft, so that smells do not
bother other passengers.

Fabulous fuselage
Much of the 747 is made
from aluminum alloy,
which is only one-third
the weight of steel.

Lots of luggage
Lockers above the seats hold
coats and carry-on luggage. The
original lockers all opened
downward, but more recently,
lockers have been made to
open upward.

*Upper
rudder*

*Lower
rudder*

Auxiliary power unit
At the very back of the aircraft is
a small gas turbine, which produces
electricity for various systems
while the aircraft is on the ground.

Toilet tanks
Flushing the toilet takes waste to collection tanks
below. A special vehicle empties the tanks when
the airplane lands.

*Economy
class*

Paintwork
Painting the fuselage of a 747
needs nearly 92 gal (350 liter) of
paint—enough to paint the insides
of more than four family houses.

Wing fuel tanks
The wing boxes support the airplane's wing and keep it rigid. In
flight, the wing boxes do another job: they are full of aviation fuel
and act as giant fuel tanks, holding 47,209 gal (178,709 liter).

Control surfaces
The ailerons on the rear of
the wings cause the aircraft
to roll when the pilot extends
them. The 747 has two sets—
one for use at high speeds, and
a second set for extra control
at low speeds.

Landing gear
The 747 has
18 landing wheels, which
tuck neatly away during flight. The
pressure in the tires is about nine
times that of an ordinary tire on a
family car.

Wonderful wings
Flexibility gives the wings their strength. The
747's wing tips can flex 26¼ ft (8 m) before
they fail totally. But the load needed to bend
the wings like this is much greater than normal.

Car factory

Some people would say that robots make ideal factory workers. They don't stop for food, they don't get sick, they don't need to sleep, and they don't get bored. They are especially suited to factories that produce many similar products, such as cars. In a car factory, robots can do almost all the repetitive and physically tiring work. They lift, assemble, weld, spray paint, and perform many other tasks.

However, robots are not good at solving problems. This factory from the 1990s needed quite a lot of humans to keep production flowing smoothly. Today's assembly lines are even more automated and need fewer humans in charge.

Press shop
The section of the factory where body and floor panels are made is called the press shop.

Roll up!
Metal for the car's panels arrives in rolls. It is coated with anti-corrosion chemicals. A remote-control crane unloads the roll from the carts.

A pressing appointment
To shape the panels, the steel passes through a series of presses, each the height of a two-story house.

Dies
The presses squash the steel sheet between dies—pairs of curved steel molds. Dies in the first press curve the metal gently. Each die that follows increases the curve. The last press squeezes the steel to the shape of the body panel and trims excess metal.

Body shop
Panels move into storage before assembly into a "body-in-white." This is a complete unpainted body, without the engine, wheels, trim, and other components.

Checking with lasers
To check that the assembly process is working perfectly, sample bodies are measured using a laser scanner. This measures the body at 350 points to ensure that it is exactly the right size.

Paint shop
It takes 25 hours to paint each body. Many different steps are needed to create a perfect finish. There isn't room to show them all, but preparation before painting requires 11 separate steps to clean the steel and provide a base for the paint.

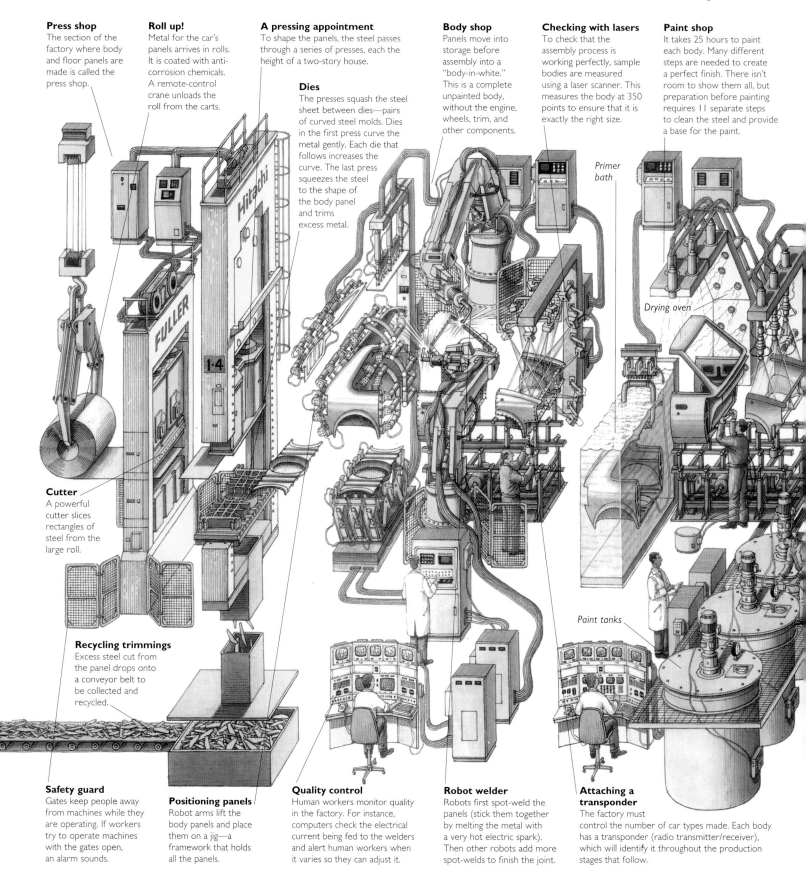

Primer bath

Drying oven

Paint tanks

Cutter
A powerful cutter slices rectangles of steel from the large roll.

Recycling trimmings
Excess steel cut from the panel drops onto a conveyor belt to be collected and recycled.

Safety guard
Gates keep people away from machines while they are operating. If workers try to operate machines with the gates open, an alarm sounds.

Positioning panels
Robot arms lift the body panels and place them on a jig—a framework that holds all the panels.

Quality control
Human workers monitor quality in the factory. For instance, computers check the electrical current being fed to the welders and alert human workers when it varies so they can adjust it.

Robot welder
Robots first spot-weld the panels (stick them together by melting the metal with a very hot electric spark). Then other robots add more spot-welds to finish the joint.

Attaching a transponder
The factory must control the number of car types made. Each body has a transponder (radio transmitter/receiver), which will identify it throughout the production stages that follow.

First dip
After careful preparation, the body plunges into a bath, which coats it with primer paint. This protects the body from corrosion and ensures that the paint will stick to it.

Bake in the oven until done
Between coats of paint, the body roasts in an oven at 180°F (82°C). After the final coat, the paint dries in an oven at 320°F (160°C).

A glossy finish
The car's transponder tells robots what color it has got to be, and the robots spray on the right paint.

Don't slam the door!
After painting, the doors are removed for the next stage. This makes access to the car interior easier and simplifies assembly of the doors.

Robo-carrier
Doors move through the production process on robo-carriers. These are miniature transport robots that move the doors along while workers add components to them. Robo-carriers also transport components around the plant, following cables buried in the floor.

Finished doors
The doors rejoin their car body as it emerges from the components/trim shop.

Components/trim shop
In this section of the factory, the car begins to look more like a car and less like a colored shell. Here, most of the electronics are added, and the passenger compartment is furnished and finished.

Fitting electronics
Small components such as lights reach the area where they are fitted on a "just-in-time" basis. Stocks of components on the production line are kept low to save space. The transponder attached to each body automatically orders the right parts as the body approaches. A robot finds the component and delivers it just in time to be fitted.

The marriage conveyor
As the car nears the end of the production process, the body is married (joined) to the engine, steering, suspension, and transmission (the gearbox and related parts).

Rolling road
Running the car on rollers allows testers to check the engine and to make sure the brakes are working.

Wax coating
One last coat of wax protects the underbody from stone chips and damage by road salt.

Valeting
Polishing gives the car its show room shine.

Trim shop
This is the only area of the factory that has not been changed by robots. Here, workers cut and stitch carpets and seats using heavy-duty sewing machines.

Overhead conveyor
Like many parts in the factory, seats move from the trim shop to the production line on overhead conveyors.

Building engines
Some parts are manufactured in this factory, but others—even whole gearboxes—may be built in factories thousands of miles away.

Fitting wheels
Workers fit the wheels by hand, but they are helped by a tool that tightens all the wheel nuts at once.

Testing, testing
Many of the car's components have been tested as they were manufactured and fitted—for example, by filling the fuel tank with air and immersing it in water to check for leaks. However, each car gets a thorough check before it goes out to be sold.

Don't forget the transponder
The transponder comes off now and goes back to the beginning of the production line.

Road test
Finally, the finished car goes off for a road test.

Helicopter

A loudspeaker at the search and rescue airbase blares, "Scramble, scramble!" and the on-duty aircrew rub their eyes and stretch to wake up. The message tells them they must go to work, and for these four men, work means saving lives. A ship is sinking, and help is needed urgently or lives may be lost.

The Sea King was one of the most effective search and rescue helicopters, and tonight's crew carefully prepare their helicopter before it speeds them to their target. At the ship, it hovers while one of the crew is lowered on a cable to pluck the sailors from the deck. Then the Sea King rushes the crew and survivors back to the airbase.

Engine fire extinguisher bottles
The pilot can fill the engine compartment with foam to extinguish a fire there.

Blade pitch control rods
Rods connect the rotor blades to the swash plate. When the swash plate moves, the angle or pitch of the rotor blades changes.

Swash plate
The pilot's controls raise and lower the swash plate and alter its angle. Raising the swash plate increases the pitch of the rotors to provide more lift. Tilting the swash plate increases the helicopter's speed or changes its direction.

Rotor

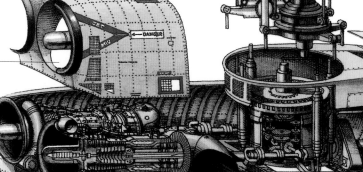

Engine air intakes

Pass the apricots, please
Objects entering the engine can cause damage, so a guard protects the air intake. Salt spray can also cause problems. One solution is to spray some engine parts with a mixture of chemicals and ground apricot stones!

Turbine
Power for the Sea King comes from two Rolls-Royce Gnome turbine engines. If one engine fails, the helicopter can return to base using the other.

Pilot
The captain of the Sea King is usually the pilot, although sometimes the radar operator or navigator is in charge of the helicopter.

Oil cooler fan

Cyclic pitch lever
Moving the cyclic pitch lever tilts the helicopter's rotor. The Sea King moves in the direction in which the rotor is tilted. For example, pushing the lever forward moves the helicopter forward.

Collective pitch lever
The controls on this lever alter both the engine speed and the pitch of the rotors. Operating them together makes the helicopter go up or down.

Co-pilot
The responsibilities of the co-pilot include navigation, preflight planning, and briefing the captain.

Yaw control
Pedals on the cabin floor control yaw—rotation of the helicopter to the left or right.

Radio and electronic equipment
Much of the helicopter's electronic equipment is mounted below the pilot and co-pilot's feet.

Radar operator
Navigation equipment and radar are the responsibility of the radar operator, who sits behind the pilot.

Fuel
With a full tank of fuel, the Sea King helicopters have a range of more than 870 miles (1,400 km).

Oxygen bottles
Every search and rescue helicopter carries a good first-aid kit, including oxygen cylinders. All members of the crew are trained in first aid.

Water wings
If the helicopter comes down over water, emergency flotation bags inflate with compressed air to prevent the helicopter from sinking.

RESCUE

Rotor blade
The rotor is the assembly on the top of the helicopter that spins around. It holds the rotor blades that make the helicopter fly by pushing down on the air underneath and creating lift. The blades also control the helicopter's direction. Tilting the rotor left and right turns the helicopter. Tilting it back and forth enables the helicopter to fly forward or even backward.

Aluminum spar
The spine of each rotor blade is a D-shaped aluminum spar. To enable the crew to check for damage to the rotor blades, the spar contains gas at high pressure. Any loss of pressure turns on a warning in the cockpit indicating that a crack has formed.

In balance
Every blade must weigh exactly the same, or the rotor will vibrate badly. Engineers insert weights into the blades to balance them.

Rotor blade core

KEY FACTS	
WESTLAND SEA KING HAR MK 3	
Length • 57¼ ft (17.43 m) (rotor folded)	
Diameter of rotor • 62 ft (18.9 m)	
Maximum range • 316¾ miles (510 km)	
Weight empty • 13,007 lb (5,900 kg)	
Maximum speed • 155¼ mph (250 kph)	

Tail rotor drive
The engine turns the tail rotor using a transmission rod that runs the length of the tail. A gearbox is needed wherever there is a bend in the transmission shaft.

Crane in the sky
The helicopter's winch enables it to lift survivors to safety. It is controlled from a panel alongside the door. There is normally room for 11 seated survivors and three stretcher cases inside the Sea King.

Winch operator
After guiding the helicopter to its target, the radar operator takes on another job, as winch operator. By giving instructions to the pilot over an intercom, the winch operator maneuvers the helicopter to exactly the right position before lowering the winchman on the end of the cable.

Tail rotor
Every helicopter has at least two rotors. If a helicopter had only one rotor, it would spin around in the air in the opposite direction to the rotor blades as soon as it left the ground. The tail rotor stops this from happening by pushing the tail sideways.

Radar scanner
The helicopter's radar system enables the crew to locate their target in the dark or in thick fog.

UHF aerial
The crew keep in touch with their base using UHF radio.

Blade pitch change mechanism
By altering the pitch of the tail rotor, the pilot can turn the helicopter in the air.

Shaft cover

Anti-collision light

Collapsible 'copter
The tail of the helicopter hinges so that it can be stowed in a small space.

Transponder
Like all aircraft, the Sea King has an automatic transponder. When radar waves from a nearby aircraft hit the transponder, is sends out a unique "Interrogation Friend or Foe" signal, which identifies the helicopter.

Floating flyer
The Sea King often carries out rescues over water, so it has a boat-shaped hull and can stay afloat on a calm sea.

Fuel intake

Life line
The winchman's life depends on a steel winch cable, so the cable gets a careful check after every mission.

Tail wheel
A nonretractable tail wheel provides a soft and stable landing for the helicopter.

Stretcher
Badly injured survivors are lifted using the Neil Robertson stretcher, named after its inventor. It has fabric flaps lined with wooden splints that keep the survivor's body immobile.

Winchman
Dangling on the end of the winch cable, the winchman is the most visible crew member. He picks up the survivors, often from the deck of a ship that may be pitching wildly in rough seas.

RAF Sea King HAR Mk3
The Westland Sea King HAR Mk3 was adapted from a Sikorsky helicopter which was first used for anti-submarine warfare in the United States. In the air-sea rescue version of the helicopter, medical supplies and stretchers took the place of rockets and depth charges. The helicopter played an important role in the Australian, British, and Indian navies.

Opera house

When you step inside an opera house, you leave reality behind. Like a magic spell, the action on the stage transports you to another land, time, or world. From the auditorium (the area where you sit and watch), operatic productions seem effortless, graceful, and glamorous. But keeping up the illusion is hard work, as an operatic production

involves singers and instrumentalists and can also include dancers and extras. An army of other workers make and paint sets, sew costumes, and sell tickets. All day long the magic spell of opera is created with paint, cloth, wood, sheets of music, and hours of tiring rehearsal.

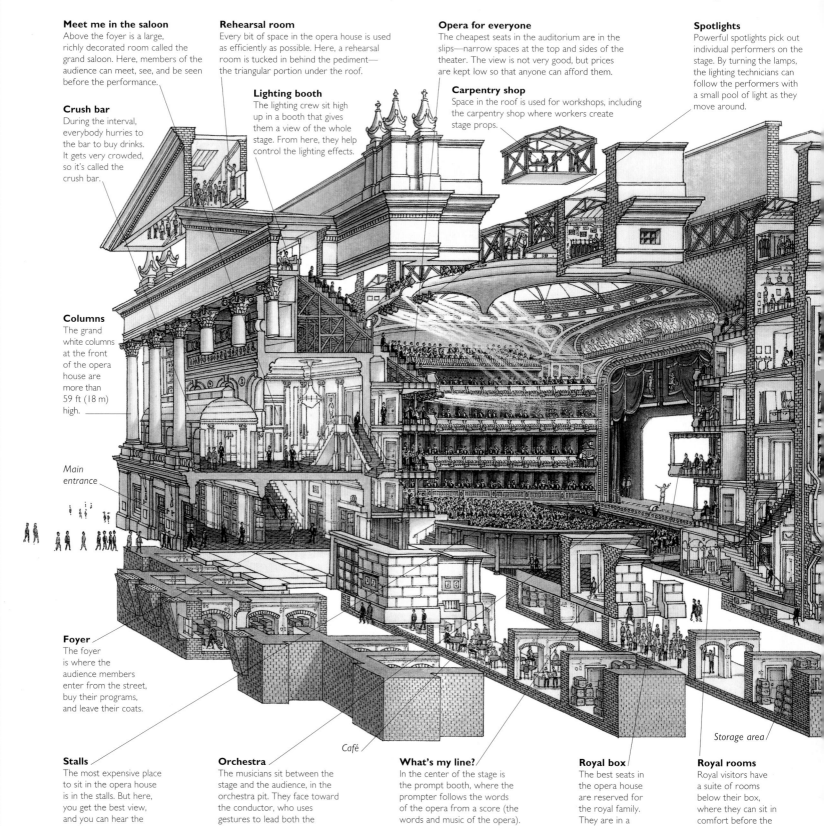

Meet me in the saloon
Above the foyer is a large, richly decorated room called the grand saloon. Here, members of the audience can meet, see, and be seen before the performance.

Crush bar
During the interval, everybody hurries to the bar to buy drinks. It gets very crowded, so it's called the crush bar.

Columns
The grand white columns at the front of the opera house are more than 59 ft (18 m) high.

Main entrance

Foyer
The foyer is where the audience members enter from the street, buy their programs, and leave their coats.

Rehearsal room
Every bit of space in the opera house is used as efficiently as possible. Here, a rehearsal room is tucked in behind the pediment—the triangular portion under the roof.

Lighting booth
The lighting crew sit high up in a booth that gives them a view of the whole stage. From here, they help control the lighting effects.

Opera for everyone
The cheapest seats in the auditorium are in the slips—narrow spaces at the top and sides of the theater. The view is not very good, but prices are kept low so that anyone can afford them.

Carpentry shop
Space in the roof is used for workshops, including the carpentry shop where workers create stage props.

Spotlights
Powerful spotlights pick out individual performers on the stage. By turning the lamps, the lighting technicians can follow the performers with a small pool of light as they move around.

Café

Storage area

Stalls
The most expensive place to sit in the opera house is in the stalls. But here, you get the best view, and you can hear the music better than anywhere else in the auditorium.

Orchestra
The musicians sit between the stage and the audience, in the orchestra pit. They face toward the conductor, who uses gestures to lead both the musicians in the pit and the performers on the stage.

What's my line?
In the center of the stage is the prompt booth, where the prompter follows the words of the opera from a score (the words and music of the opera). If anyone forgets their words, the prompter reminds them.

Royal box
The best seats in the opera house are reserved for the royal family. They are in a private box at the side of the stage.

Royal rooms
Royal visitors have a suite of rooms below their box, where they can sit in comfort before the performance and during the interval.

A supporting role
Eight huge girders support the roof. Each weighs 33 tons (30 tonnes). The girders were prefabricated (constructed separately from the rest of the building) in a factory 105 miles (170 km) from the opera house.

Lighting
Powerful lamps hang from gantries (long hanging racks) above the stage.

Costume storage
Designing and making costumes is a huge task: everybody in the cast has at least one costume.

Painting room
Because backdrops are so big, there is a huge room for painting them. This one is for Verdi's opera *Aida*, set in Ancient Egypt.

Chorus rehearsal room
A choir, called the chorus, sing some of the opera on their own, and also sometimes accompany the opera soloists. The chorus practice in a large room at the back of the building.

Score store
Every member of the cast needs a copy of the words and music of the opera, and there is a different part for each musical instrument in the orchestra. So the opera house has a library containing all the different parts for many operas.

Ballet practice room
The ballet dancers must practice for many hours a day to keep their bodies supple. They have a rehearsal room high up behind the stage.

Royal Opera House, Covent Garden

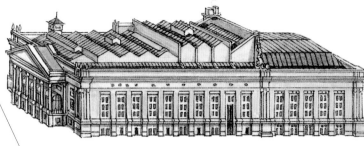

The Royal Opera House in London, England—home to the Royal Ballet, too—is more than 150 years old, and replaced an older building burned down by a fire. In 1997–1999, the building house was completely renovated, so the Royal Opera House looks pretty different today.

Ballet dancers practicing

Fan club
Opera fans wait at the stage door after a show hoping for a glimpse of their heroes leaving.

Foundations

A big noise
Down below the stage is a big room where the orchestra rehearse and where they store large instruments such as harps and pianos.

Flip on a light
To control the stage lights, there is a lighting board at the sides of the stage. From here, the electricians can switch the lights on and off at the correct moment.

Switch room
The opera house uses a lot of electricity, and the switch room controls its distribution.

Trap
The stage has five traps, or small elevators. To make a sudden appearance, a performer stands on a lowered trap beneath the stage. On cue (at the right instant in the production), stage hands operate the trap, and the performer is hoisted rapidly upward to stage level.

Elevator
The opera house is nine stories high, so an elevator is essential.

Gentlemen's chorus dressing room

Ladies' chorus dressing room
The members of the chorus all share a big dressing room. The costume staff have to start early in the day, washing, repairing, and pressing the many costumes.

Solo artists' dressing rooms
Only solo singers, or principals, have a dressing room all to themselves. The rooms are tiny, but well-known opera stars have a suite of rooms— a dressing room, and a sitting room where they can entertain friends and fans.

Steam train

When steam trains first appeared, around 1830, they were as exciting as space travel is today. They terrified some people, who feared for their health. One writer commented: *"What can be more ridiculous than locomotives traveling twice as fast as stage coaches? We should as soon expect people to suffer themselves to be fired off on rockets as trust themselves to the mercy of a machine going at such a rate."* Pleading for sanity, he demanded that railway trains should be limited to a speed of 8 or 9 miles an hour. Others declared that locomotives would *"kill the birds, prevent cows from grazing and hens from laying, burn houses, and cause the extinction of the race of horses."* All these critics were proved wrong, and by the middle of the 20th century, the steam train reigned as the most sophisticated way of traveling by land. Pullman passengers (those traveling in the most luxurious class) could enjoy an invigorating shower, eat a first-class meal, or watch the latest film in the train's movie theater.

Locomotive

The locomotive shown here belonged to England's London and North Eastern Railway. It was numbered 4472 and named *Flying Scotsman*. It is a "Pacific" class locomotive—a typical passenger express locomotive of the 1920s and 1930s. "Pacific" class locomotives had a set of six large linked driving wheels in the center, with four free running wheels in front and two free running wheels at the rear.

Side view showing wheel arrangement

Bird's-eye view

A torrent of steam and smoke would normally have hidden the locomotive from view as it passed under bridges. The 10 tons (9 tonnes) of coal in the tender was used as fuel for nonstop journeys.

Top view of locomotive and tender

LNER

1

RESTAUR

Side view of restaurant carriage

Flying Scotsman train

Both a locomotive and a train were called *Flying Scotsman*. The *Flying Scotsman* express train traveled from London, England, to Edinburgh, Scotland—a distance of 392¾ miles (631.9 km). It traveled nonstop from May 1928, making it then the longest nonstop service in the world.

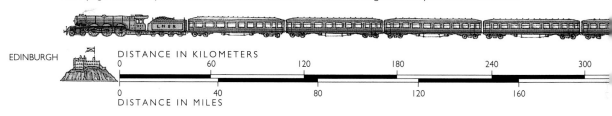

EDINBURGH

DISTANCE IN KILOMETERS					
0	60	120	180	240	300

DISTANCE IN MILES				
0	40	80	120	160

Ten-car set
Carriages were coupled in sets of 8, 10, 12, or even 14. *The carriages shown here are a selection to show the types of travel available to passengers in the 1930s. They do not represent an actual train make-up.*

KEY FACTS	
FLYING SCOTSMAN LOCOMOTIVE	
Length without tender • 43 ft (13.1 m)	
Width over footplate • 9 ft (2.74 m)	
Height to top of cab • 12¾ ft (3.9 m)	
Driving wheel diameter • 80 in (203 cm)	
Maximum weight • 105 tons (96 tonnes)	
Tractive effort • 36,464 lb (16,540 kg)	

Traveling Post Office (TPO)
The railway was a vital link in the mail distribution network. On some trains, postmen sorted letters during the journey to reduce delivery time.

Carriage construction
In the 1930s, steel carriages began to supersede the older wooden types. Sometimes the steel was painted to look like wood.

Guard's van
Luggage that did not fit in the carriages traveled in the guard's van.

Line-side mail gantry
The Traveling Post Office could pick up mail bags without stopping. Post office workers hung mail bags on a line-side gantry (support), and a special hook collected them as the train passed.

Hairdressing saloon
Both men and women could have their hair trimmed and styled on the train, and there was a waiting room so that passengers could wait in comfort.

Lavatory
Flushing discharged the contents of the toilet bowl onto the track below, so maintenance staff walked alongside the rails, not between them.

Who was on board

Express trains in the 1930s had a large complement of staff. The driver and fireman drove the locomotive. The guard looked after luggage and safe departures. The ticket inspector made sure everyone traveled in the right class of carriage. Stewards served the meals that the cooks prepared. The barber looked after the passengers' hairdressing requirements, and the projectionist showed films in the movie theater car. Finally, post office staff sorted mail in the TPO.

The Crew

Driver   *Fireman*   *Guard*

Ticket Inspector   *Cooks*

Stewards   *Buffet Steward*

Projectionist   *Barber*   *Post Office Staff*

The Passengers

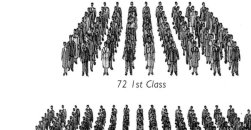

72 1st Class

255 3rd Class

Front view showing smokebox door

Footplate

The controls of the locomotive are on the footplate. The driver's view ahead was often obscured by steam or smoke. The fireman fed the fire with coal. He also had to learn the train's route so he would know when to stoke up the fire to provide more power.

Tender

Steam locomotives ran on coal and water. The locomotive's tender carried a supply of both. It also had a corridor that allowed a relief crew to walk through and replace the driver and fireman without stopping.

Footplate view showing controls

Looking up

This is the view that the maintenance crew had in the engine shed when they crawled underneath the locomotive to remove ash from the firebox grate.

Bottom view of locomotive and tender

Carriages

Carriages were built by skilled workers, mainly using a framework of teak wood. By the 1930s, when the carriage shown above was built, many parts were made of steel. Some later steel-shelled carriages were then painted to look like teak.

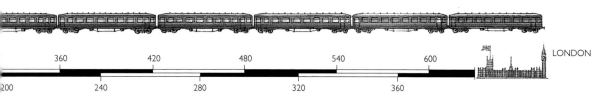

LONDON

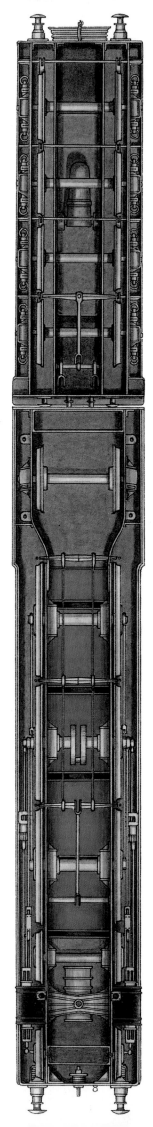

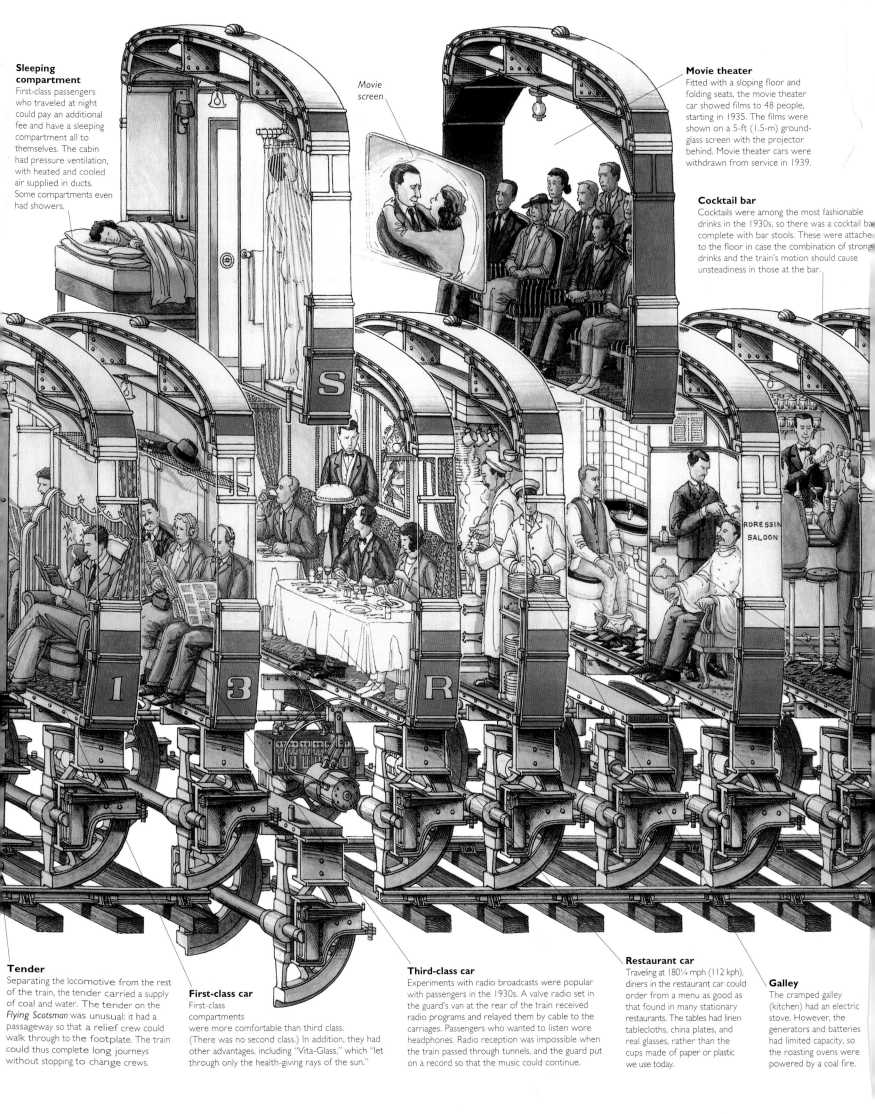

Sleeping compartment
First-class passengers who traveled at night could pay an additional fee and have a sleeping compartment all to themselves. The cabin had pressure ventilation, with heated and cooled air supplied in ducts. Some compartments even had showers.

Movie screen

Movie theater
Fitted with a sloping floor and folding seats, the movie theater car showed films to 48 people, starting in 1935. The films were shown on a 5-ft (1.5-m) ground-glass screen with the projector behind. Movie theater cars were withdrawn from service in 1939.

Cocktail bar
Cocktails were among the most fashionable drinks in the 1930s, so there was a cocktail bar complete with bar stools. These were attached to the floor in case the combination of strong drinks and the train's motion should cause unsteadiness in those at the bar.

Tender
Separating the locomotive from the rest of the train, the tender carried a supply of coal and water. The tender on the *Flying Scotsman* was unusual: it had a passageway so that a relief crew could walk through to the footplate. The train could thus complete long journeys without stopping to change crews.

First-class car
First-class compartments were more comfortable than third class. (There was no second class.) In addition, they had other advantages, including "Vita-Glass," which "let through only the health-giving rays of the sun."

Third-class car
Experiments with radio broadcasts were popular with passengers in the 1930s. A valve radio set in the guard's van at the rear of the train received radio programs and relayed them by cable to the carriages. Passengers who wanted to listen wore headphones. Radio reception was impossible when the train passed through tunnels, and the guard put on a record so that the music could continue.

Restaurant car
Traveling at 180¼ mph (112 kph), diners in the restaurant car could order from a menu as good as that found in many stationary restaurants. The tables had linen tablecloths, china plates, and real glasses, rather than the cups made of paper or plastic we use today.

Galley
The cramped galley (kitchen) had an electric stove. However, the generators and batteries had limited capacity, so the roasting ovens were powered by a coal fire.

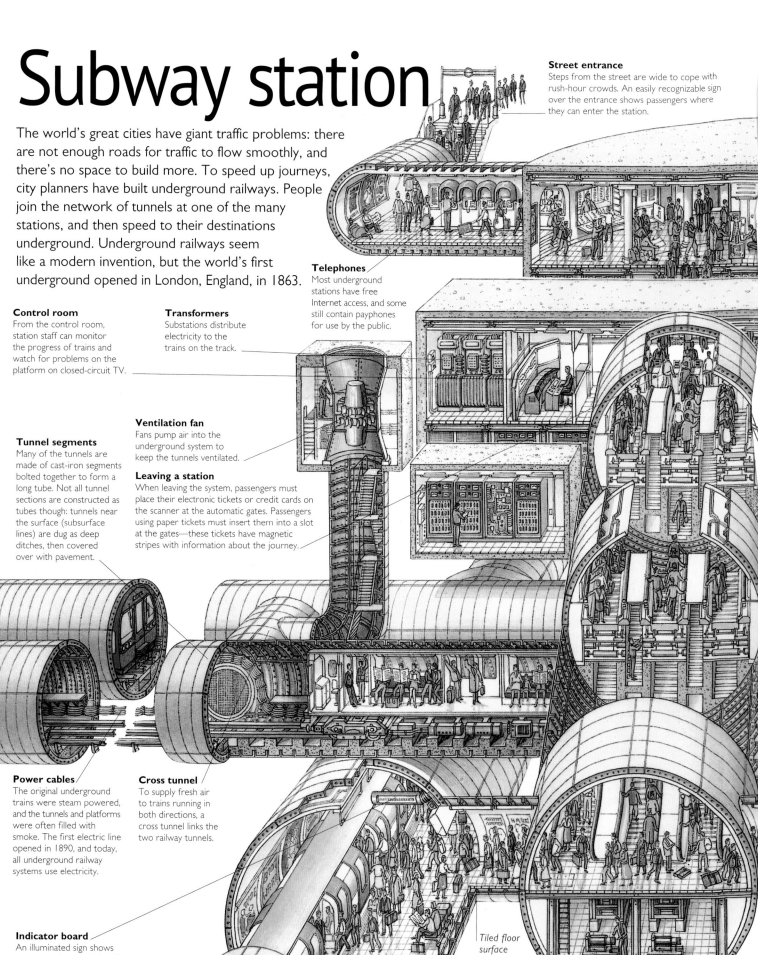

0

Subway station

The world's great cities have giant traffic problems: there are not enough roads for traffic to flow smoothly, and there's no space to build more. To speed up journeys, city planners have built underground railways. People join the network of tunnels at one of the many stations, and then speed to their destinations underground. Underground railways seem like a modern invention, but the world's first underground opened in London, England, in 1863.

Street entrance
Steps from the street are wide to cope with rush-hour crowds. An easily recognizable sign over the entrance shows passengers where they can enter the station.

Telephones
Most underground stations have free Internet access, and some still contain payphones for use by the public.

Control room
From the control room, station staff can monitor the progress of trains and watch for problems on the platform on closed-circuit TV.

Transformers
Substations distribute electricity to the trains on the track.

Ventilation fan
Fans pump air into the underground system to keep the tunnels ventilated.

Tunnel segments
Many of the tunnels are made of cast-iron segments bolted together to form a long tube. Not all tunnel sections are constructed as tubes though: tunnels near the surface (subsurface lines) are dug as deep ditches, then covered over with pavement.

Leaving a station
When leaving the system, passengers must place their electronic tickets or credit cards on the scanner at the automatic gates. Passengers using paper tickets must insert them into a slot at the gates—these tickets have magnetic stripes with information about the journey.

Power cables
The original underground trains were steam powered, and the tunnels and platforms were often filled with smoke. The first electric line opened in 1890, and today, all underground railway systems use electricity.

Cross tunnel
To supply fresh air to trains running in both directions, a cross tunnel links the two railway tunnels.

Indicator board
An illuminated sign shows passengers how long they have to wait for the next train.

Rails
In addition to the two rails on which the train wheels run, there are two more rails to provide electric power to the trains.

Tiled floor surface

Tunnel depth
Tube tunnels are about 82 ft (25 m) underground. Subsurface lines (those in covered trenches) are not nearly so deep though: most are less than 24½ ft (7.5 m) down. Not all of London's underground railway is actually below the ground: outside the city center, the trains run on the surface.

Ticket office
Station staff issue tickets for people who do not have change for ticket machines or who want season tickets.

Route map
Passengers find their way around with the aid of a color-coded map.

Shops and kiosks
Retailers rent kiosks and small shops at the stations to sell things that travelers need. Rent from the shops helps subsidize, or reduce, the fares.

Staff rest area
More than 20,000 people work for the London Underground. Staff have rest areas with toilets and washing facilities, and a few stations also have canteens.

Automatic gates
Placing an electronic ticket or credit card on the scanner at the automatic gates opens them, allowing the passenger to go down to the platform. There are also slots in the gates for traditional paper tickets.

Escalator motor

Escalator
Escalators carry passengers up and down the sloping tunnels. Some escalators work 24 hours a day. A step on the average escalator travels about 466,028 miles (750,000 km) over its 40-year lifespan—the same distance from Earth to the moon and back.

A long way to walk
The longest escalator on the London Underground lifts passengers nearly 92 ft (28 m).

Tunnel songs
Buskers play to get money from passengers. There are selected places in the network of stations where performers can sing or play an instrument.

Emergency stairs
Some stations have emergency staircases so that passengers can escape if a fire blocks the escalator. Extra staircases are also needed for maintenance purposes.

See yourself on TV
Train drivers must make sure that everyone boards the train safely. TV cameras monitor the crowds, and the driver watches a screen at one end of the platform close to the cab. Cameras are also linked to the control room for passenger safety.

Staircase
At most stations, there are some steps in the passages and corridors leading to the platform.

Sliding doors
Sliding doors open when the train reaches a station. As a safety precaution, the train cannot take off unless all the doors are tightly closed.

Standing room only
There isn't space for everyone to sit down, so many passengers stand up, especially on short journeys. They hold on to straps and rails so that they don't fall over when the train stops and starts.

Carriages
Older trains are usually made up of eight separate cars, while modern trains have walk-through carriages. More than 1,000 people can squeeze onto a train during the rush hour.

KEY FACTS LONDON UNDERGROUND	
Track length in system	249¾ miles (402 km)
Track length underground	103¾ miles (167 km)
Average speed of trains	20½ mph (33 kph)
Deepest tunnel	221 ft (67.4 m) below ground
Passenger journeys a year	1.34 billion
Number of stations	270
Passengers per day at busiest station	261,000

Fishing trawler

Before farming began, people got their food by gathering grains and fruits and by hunting wild animals. Today, much of our food comes from farms and fishing. Modern fishing ships are mechanized and catch almost everything in their path. Sadly, their success has sometimes led to overfishing, and today there are strict regulations to prevent this.

Radar scanners
The rotating radar scanners enable the crew to detect other vessels many miles away, even when thick fog reduces visibility.

Radio mast

Fishing lights
Fishing nets are a hazard to other vessels, so when fishing at night, the trawler displays special warning lights.

Bow gantry
The ship's two gantries support tackle that helps haul in the nets. The front of a ship is called the bow, so this is the bow gantry.

Cable winch
A small winch below the bow gantry pulls the cables that move the nets around on deck.

Pulleys
Pulleys strung between the gantries enable the crew to move the catch (the net full of fish) around the deck.

Net drum
As it is emptied of f
a net is wound onto
the net drum for
storage.

Reflector compass
The ship's compass on the top of the wheelhouse contains an optical system so that the bearing (the direction in which the ship is heading) can be seen clearly by the crew member steering the ship.

Radio room
The radio keeps the ship in contact with shore personnel. Many skippers prefer not to use the radio when they find good fishing grounds, because they fear that other ships will locate the spot from the radio signal.

Hydraulic trawl winches
When the ship is towing the trawl, the crew use two large winches to pay out and haul in the trawl warps (the cables attached to the net).

Skipper
The master or captain of a trawler is called the skipper.

Wheelhouse
From the wheelhouse, the helm has a good all-around view of the decks and of the sea on all sides.

Searchlight

Life preserver
Stern trawlers are safer than the older side trawlers, but life preservers are still vital in case any of the crew fall overboard.

Galley (kitchen)

Accommodations
Space is very limited on the ship, and none of the crew has a large cabin, but the skipper and mate (his assistant) have a little more space.

Skipper's accommodation

Mate's accommodation

Crew accommodation

Anchor windlass
A power windlass (winch) hauls in the anchor when the ship moves from the fishing grounds.

Anchor
The ship has two anchors—one on each side of the hull.

Anchor windlass machinery

Anchor chain locker
The long anchor chain is stored in here when it is hauled in by the windlass.

Water ballast tank
When the ship is not fully loaded, water in the ballast tank keeps it on an even keel (level in the sea). As the crew catch and load fish, water is pumped out of the ballast to compensate for the extra weight on board.

Rib construction
The ship must be strong to withstand the ice and high seas of the Arctic fishing grounds. So the steel plates of the hull are welded to a structure of ribs.

Freshwater tanks

Chart room
Ocean maps are called charts. They show the coastline, depth of the water and features such as lighthouses.

Oil tanks

Engine control room
Sound insulation absorbs the noise from the engines, so the control room is fairly quiet.

Recreation room

Mess room
The crew grab meals in the mess room during breaks in the fishing.

Electronics room
Fishing vessels have many navigational aids. Electronic instruments monitor signals from land beacons or orbiting satellites to give the ship's position to within about 328 ft (100 m). Sonar and echo sounding equipment help the crew locate schools of fish.

Boiler

Fuel oil tanks

Engine room
The 2,500-horsepower main engine can power the ship forward at up to 14 knots (16 mph/25.93 kph).

KEY FACTS

Length	196¾ ft (60 m)
Breadth	37¾ ft (11.5 m)
Weight	1,036 tons (940 tonnes)
Freezing capacity	27 tons (25 tonnes)/day
Hold capacity	660 tons (600 tonnes)

Fishing Trawler

Trawlers fish by towing a net bag, or trawl, behind them as they move forward through the water. The stern trawler, shown here, developed in the 1950s from the whaling ships, which had ramps at the stern to haul whale carcasses on board. Onboard freezing plants, which became commonplace in the 1960s, made it possible for fishing vessels to make much longer trips because the frozen catch did not spoil while at sea.

Deck hands
On the deck, the crew wear waterproof coats and hats (called sou'westers after the cold southwesterly winds) and rubber boots. According to superstitious fisherfolk from Whitby on England's east coast, a fisherman joining his ship must carry his boots under his arm. Carrying them over his shoulder brings bad luck to the ship.

Fish washing machine
After gutting, the catch is washed to remove blood and traces of offal (fish guts).

Gutting machine
Gutting used to be done by hand on deck, but machines have now taken over this unpleasant task.

Ramp
The ship is called a stern trawler because the crew winch the net in up a ramp at the stern (rear). Older ships are often called sidewinders because the net has to be hauled in over the side. Fishing crews prefer stern trawlers because they are safer, and because the deck where the crew work is not so exposed to the freezing wind and sea.

Cod end
When the net is full of fish, it is hauled on board, and the fish collect at the "cod end"—the closed end of the net. Once the catch has been hauled on board, the crew untie the cod end and lift it. The fish slide down to the factory area on a lower deck.

Seagulls
Fishing vessels often gather a following of seagulls, which eat the fish offal thrown overboard. Superstitious sailors believe that three seagulls flying together overhead are a sign of death.

Trawl towing blocks
There are two sets of towing blocks (apparatus for towing the nets at the ship's stern). The trawl warps pass over one set of blocks for bottom trawling (fishing on the sea bed); they are moved to the other set for midwater trawling (fishing between the surface and the sea bed).

Otter boards
For bottom trawling, a pair of otter boards is attached to the net. The water passing between the boards forces them apart, keeping the mouth of the net open.

Ramp

Trawl net store
The ship carries spare nets in case one set is lost at sea. A locker at the stern of the ship keeps the bulky nets safe and out of the way.

Fish hold
At the heart of the ship is the fish hold, a giant cold store that keeps the catch frozen in solid blocks at -4°F (-20°C) for transport back to the shore.

Vertical plate freezer
The ship's freezer freezes fish into blocks weighing about 110 lb (50 kg). It can handle about 27 tons (25 tonnes) a day.

Conveyor
Frozen fish blocks move from the factory area to the fish hold along a conveyor.

Removing frozen fish
Freezing takes about an hour, then the crew remove the solid blocks of fish and load them onto the conveyor leading to the fish hold.

Deheading machine
Fish to be sold at fish shops is frozen whole, but much of the catch will go for processing into prepared fish products. To save space in storage, these fish have their heads removed at the start of processing.

Fish chute
In the factory area, fish slide down a chute onto a conveyor.

Propeller
Blades on the propeller have variable pitch: their angle can be changed to control the ship's speed.

Cod liver oil tank
Gutting and filleting fish creates a lot of by-products, and this ship has a large tank that can store more than 44 tons (40 tonnes) of cod liver oil.

Steering gear compartment
Apparatus in the steering gear compartment operates the rudder, controlling the course (direction) of the ship.

Empire State Building

Not long ago, cities looked very different, because until about 1880, few buildings rose higher than five floors. One reason for this was the stairs: nobody wanted to walk any higher. Another obstacle was the thickness of the walls, which had to support the great weight of the building. The invention of the safety elevator by Elisha Otis (1811–1861) in 1852 solved the first problem. The second was solved when stronger steel replaced weaker cast iron starting in the 1870s. It then became possible to give buildings a strong frame to carry the weight of every floor. The walls no longer took the weight, so they could be thin and light, or even made of glass.

Office space
To ensure that natural daylight reaches everywhere, no office space is farther than 27¾ ft (8.5 m) from a window. This was a rule laid down when the building was commissioned (ordered) and the architect took great care to follow it. The appearance of the Empire State Building might have been very different if bigger rooms had been allowed.

Central service core
Much of the ingenuity that went into the design of the building was spent planning the central core that rises from the ground to the top floor. The core carries the elevators and all the services, such as electricity, telephones, air conditioning, and plumbing.

Mail room
The building is so vast that it needs its own post office. Here, in the mail room, workers sort mail that is delivered by chutes from every floor.

Piles
More than 200 piles (columns driven into the ground) support the weight of the Empire State Building. The piles, made of steel and concrete, rest directly on the bedrock 32¾ ft (10 m) below street level.

Bedrock
New York was the original skyscraper city. Manhattan Island at its center is made of granite, which provides a solid foundation for the many massively heavy buildings.

Foundation level
To dig the foundations, workers removed rock and soil amounting to three quarters of the weight of the Empire State Building itself.

Water
To raise water to the top of the building requires pumps with tremendous power. 62 miles (100 km) of pipe channel the water from the pumps to every floor.

Electrical switchgear
Tenants of the building consume enough power every year to supply a city of 11,000 inhabitants. There are transformers in the basement and on the 84th floor.

Observatory
From the viewing platform on the 102nd floor, visitors can see more than 77 miles (125 km) on a clear day. Three and a half million people a year come to see the view, but many are disappointed, because mist often shrouds the building.

TV mast
The tip of the 203½-ft (62-m) TV mast that tops off the Empire State Building is 1,453½ ft (443 m) above the ground.

Observation windows
Because high winds sweep upward around the building, visitors sometimes see rain and snow falling upward.

Airship mooring mast
The original owners of the Empire State Building planned an airship mooring mast for the top. In the days before passenger aircraft, everyone thought that airships (huge passenger balloons) would soon be flying regularly from Europe to the United States. However, landing airships on the mast proved to be highly dangerous, and the idea was abandoned.

elevator motors

Express elevators
The fastest elevators whisk sightseers to the observation galleries at speeds of more than 1,148 ft (350 m) a minute.

Cleaners
The window cleaners work from cradles that hang from winches running around the roof of the 80th floor. Each of the building's 6,500 windows is cleaned every month. The job is made more difficult by high winds that make the water trickle up the window instead of down.

Stairs
There are 1,860 steps from street level to the 102nd floor.

Inter-floor structure
Floors are constructed like sandwiches, with space in between for cables, telephone lines, and pipes.

Storage areas

Elevator motors
The positioning of the elevators was vital to the building's success. Too few, and tenants could not get to their offices quickly enough. But each new elevator reduces the amount of office space to let. In the end, 73 elevators were built.

Steel floor frame
A network of horizontal steel girders built first provided a firm support for the concrete floors that were poured on top and left to harden. Even at the time, the frame was unnecessarily heavy—today, only half the weight of steel would be used.

Beacons
The Empire State Building has beacons to warn aircraft of its height, but on July 28, 1945, a fog-bound plane crashed into the building between the 78th and 79th floors. A typewriter mechanic, Alf Spalthoff, saw the crash as he ate a tuna sandwich in a café not far away. He said: "When it hit, there was a big explosion that seemed to come from four or five of the floors at once."

Curtain wall
The Empire State Building was designed as a framework, with an outside shell called a curtain wall to keep the weather out and the people in. Most of the wall panels were prefabricated—cut to size or assembled elsewhere—so that they could be installed rapidly.

Wall panels
The shimmering vertical lines of the building's exterior are created by stainless-steel panels. The lines draw the eye upward, making the building look taller.

Brick lining
When the curtain wall was fitted in place, workers lined the inside of each floor with bricks—10 million of them for the whole building.

Concrete floor

Tall tale
The Empire State Building in New York City is the world's best-known skyscraper. Opened on May 1, 1931, it was for many years the world's tallest building. It was the creation of a group of business tycoons led by John Jakob Raskob. His aim was to commission the most beautiful skyscraper ever built—but also to make a lot of money by renting out the office space in the building, which stands on one of the city's most desirable sites.

Get it up quickly
The Empire State Building was completed in record time: 3,000 workers labored daily for less than 15 months to finish it. But in the rush to construct the building, 14 workers died in accidents.

Tenants' offices
The Empire State Building is an office block, with office space rented out to tenants. When the building opened during the Great Depression, business in the United States was very bad, and the owners were at first able to rent only a quarter of the offices. New Yorkers dubbed it "The Empty State Building."

Power cables
More than 372 miles (600 km) of cable supply power and light to office tenants.

Main entrance
The Empire State Building is constructed so that the main door opens onto Fifth Avenue, New York's most fashionable street.

Lobby
Inside the main door, a magnificent lobby rises three stories high. On the walls are paintings of the seven great wonders of the world—and one of the Empire State Building, which the owners modestly claimed was the eighth wonder, and the only one built in the 20th century.

Office workers
15,000 people work in the Empire State Building.

Parking space

Electrical gear

Utilities
Conduits, pipes, and cables under the street supply the building with gas, phone lines, water, steam, and electricity.

Steel skeleton
Building the Empire State Building's supporting framework required 63,934 tons (58,000 tonnes) of steel. 300 steelworkers completed the frame in 23 weeks.

Building materials
If a single train had brought all the building materials to the site, the guard's van would have been more than 56 miles (90 km) away when the engine arrived.

Cleaners
When the office workers have gone home, 150 cleaners vacuum and dust.

Waste disposal plant
Cleaners empty paper trash into sacks and carry it to the basement in the service elevators. The waste is stored for a day in case someone throws valuable papers away and needs to sort through the garbage. After 24 hours, the waste is compacted into bales weighing nearly half a ton and removed.

Air conditioning
Large buildings would be uncomfortable to work in without special heating and ventilation systems. The Empire State Building is air conditioned by more than 5,511 tons (5,000 tonnes) of equipment in the basement, which pumps chilled water to air conditioning units in every office. The air inside the building changes six times an hour.

KEY FACTS

Height • 1,453½ ft (443 m) (including TV mast)	
Weight • 339,511 tons (308,000 tonnes)	
Ground area • 83,743 sq ft (7,780 sq m)	
Volume • 37¾ million cu ft (1.05 million cu m)	
Floors • 102	
Stairs to top • 1,860	

Space Shuttle

For centuries, people dreamed of space travel. The dream came true in 1961, when space flights with human crews began. But space vehicles were very expensive, and only a tiny part of each returned to Earth. The rest remained in orbit (floating weightless in space) as hazardous "space junk."

The space shuttle was the first reusable space vehicle—like other spacecraft, it launched into orbit on the back of a rocket, but glided back to Earth at the end of the mission, to be used again. Space shuttles completed 133 successful missions between 1981 and 2011.

Where's the bathroom?
Washing was not easy on the orbiter, because without gravity, water couldn't flow down; instead, it went everywhere and could damage delicate equipment. To wash hands, there was a device like a goldfish bowl. A constant flow of air through the handholes controlled the water inside. To wash faces and bodies, the crew used washcloths.

Heatproof tiles
When the orbiter reentered the Earth's atmosphere, the friction (rubbing) of the air rushing past slowed it down. However, the friction heated the orbiter to a very high temperature. To protect the craft, it was covered in 24,192 ceramic heatproof tiles. Each was individually made, and no two tiles were the same.

Taking up arms
Because there is no gravity in space, a delicately jointed arm was able to do jobs that required a huge crane on Earth. The remote manipulator arm moved in many directions, so that it could lift satellites and other payloads (cargoes) in the cargo bay.

Payload assist module
A small rocket engine, called the payload assist module, powered the satellite into a higher orbit as soon as it was a safe distance from the orbiter.

Radiator
The apparatus on board the orbiter generated a large amount of heat. A cooling system similar to that in a refrigerator took the heat to radiators fitted to the cargo bay doors. From there, the heat dispersed into space.

The shuttle orbiter

The section of the space shuttle housing the crew and cargo compartments was called the orbiter. At launch, the orbiter was dwarfed by a huge external fuel tank and two solid-fuel rocket boosters. The orbiter discarded these parts less than 10 minutes after leaving the ground.

Vertical stabilizer
Like the fin of an aircraft, the vertical stabilizer kept the shuttle on course in Earth's atmosphere and helped it steer.

Main engine nozzle
Burning liquid hydrogen and oxygen in these nozzles gave the orbiter the power it needed to lift off into space. After lift-off, these engines were not used again on the mission.

Rear rockets
External pods on either side of the orbiter fuselage contained the rocket engines and fuel supply that the craft used to maneuver (change speed and position) in space.

Orbital maneuvering system (OMS) engines
The crew would fire the OMS engines to make major changes to the orbiter's speed and direction in space.

Smart system
The reaction control system (RCS) made small changes in the position of the orbiter. There were 44 small rocket engines in the RCS, and they were fired by the autopilot. Tiny engines called vernier thrusters fine-tuned space maneuvers.

Fuel and oxidizer supplies
Ball-shaped tanks held the fuel for the OMS and RCS engines. In addition to the fuel tank, there was a separate supply of oxidizer—without this, the fuel would not burn.

Wing sections
The orbiter's wings were constructed in a similar way to those of an aircraft, with a framework of aluminum spars and ribs.

Auxiliary power unit fuel

Cargo bay door

Going down?
When the orbiter was landing, the crew used movable sections of the wing, called elevons, to control the craft's glide back to the ground.

Wonderful wheels
As the orbiter approached the landing site, the pilot pressed a button on the flightdeck to extend the landing gear (landing wheels).

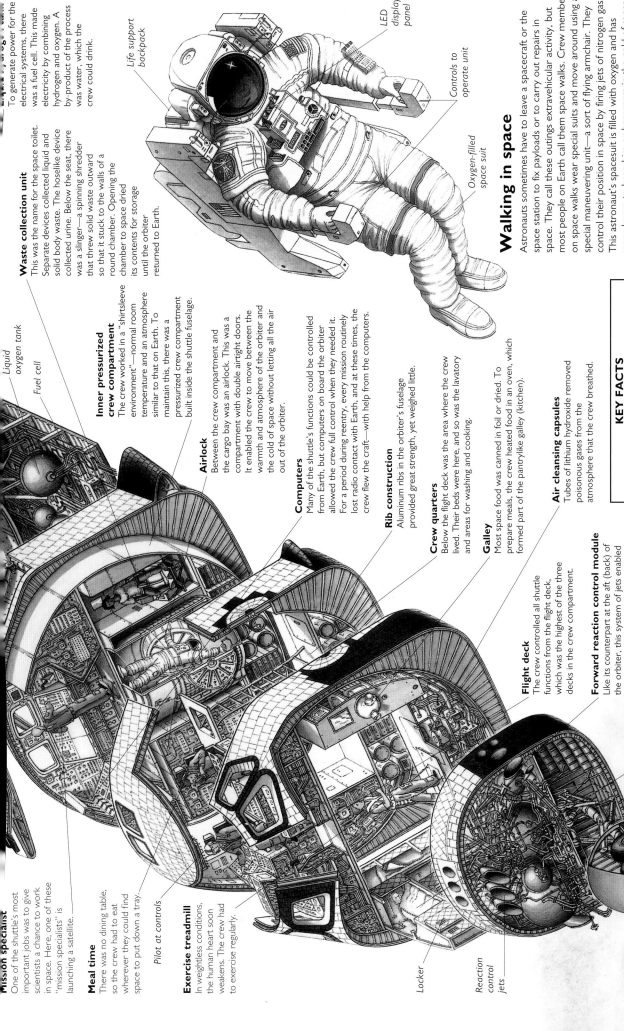

To generate power for the electrical systems, there was a fuel cell. This made electricity by combining hydrogen and oxygen. A by-product of the process was water, which the crew could drink.

Life support backpack

LED display panel

Controls to operate unit

Oxygen-filled space suit

Waste collection unit

This was the name for the space toilet. Separate devices collected liquid and solid body waste. The hoselike device collected urine. Below the seat, there was a slinger—a spinning shredder that threw solid waste outward so that it stuck to the walls of a round chamber. Opening the chamber to space dried its contents for storage until the orbiter returned to Earth.

Walking in space

Astronauts sometimes have to leave a spacecraft or the space station to fix payloads or to carry out repairs in space. They call these outings extravehicular activity, but most people on Earth call them space walks. Crew members on space walks wear special suits and move around using a special maneuvering unit—a sort of flying armchair. They control their position in space by firing jets of nitrogen gas. This astronaut's spacesuit is filled with oxygen and has many layers to keep him or her warm in the cold of space. A backpack life support unit filters harmful gases from the air the astronaut breathes and keeps the suit at a comfortable temperature. A chest-mounted LED display panel keeps the astronaut informed about factors such as fuel and battery status.

Inner pressurized crew compartment

The crew worked in a "shirtsleeve environment"—normal room temperature and an atmosphere similar to that on Earth. To maintain this, there was a pressurized crew compartment built inside the shuttle fuselage.

Airlock

Between the crew compartment and the cargo bay was an airlock. This was a compartment with double airtight doors. It enabled the crew to move between the warmth and atmosphere of the orbiter and the cold of space without letting all the air out of the orbiter.

Computers

Many of the shuttle's functions could be controlled from Earth, but computers on board the orbiter allowed the crew full control when they needed it. For a period during reentry, every mission routinely lost radio contact with Earth, and at these times, the crew flew the craft—with help from the computers.

Rib construction

Aluminum ribs in the orbiter's fuselage provided great strength, yet weighed little.

Crew quarters

Below the flight deck was the area where the crew lived. Their beds were here, and so was the lavatory and areas for washing and cooking.

Galley

Most space food was canned in foil or dried. To prepare meals, the crew heated food in an oven, which formed part of the pantrylike galley (kitchen).

Air cleansing capsules

Tubes of lithium hydroxide removed poisonous gases from the atmosphere that the crew breathed.

Flight deck

The crew controlled all shuttle functions from the flight deck, which was the highest of the three decks in the crew compartment.

Forward reaction control module

Like its counterpart at the aft (back) of the orbiter, this system of jets enabled the orbiter to maneuver in space.

Sleep stations

There is no gravity in space, so beds (or "sleep stations") didn't need to be padded—straps held the crew gently against a panel.

Nose cone

The nose landing gear was stowed in the nose cone during the mission, extending only when the orbiter was ready to land.

Liquid oxygen tank

Fuel cell

Mission specialist

One of the shuttle's most important jobs was to give scientists a chance to work in space. Here, one of these "mission specialists" is launching a satellite.

Meal time

There was no dining table, so the crew had to eat wherever they could find space to put down a tray.

Pilot at controls

Exercise treadmill

In weightless conditions, the human heart soon weakens. The crew had to exercise regularly.

Locker

Reaction control jets

Reinforced carbon-carbon

The orbiter nose cone and the leading edges of the wings were constructed of a material called reinforced carbon-carbon. This immensely strong material can withstand temperatures of 3,002°F (1,650°C).

KEY FACTS

Length of orbiter • 122 ft (37.2 m)

Wingspan • 78 ft (23.8 m)

Overall launch length (including solid fuel booster) • 183¼ ft (56 m)

Weight • 178,287¾ lb (80,870 kg)

Payload bay area of orbiter • 15 ft (4.6 m) x 60 ft (18.3 m)

Cargo capacity • 55,000 lb (24,948 kg)

INCREDIBLE CROSS-SECTIONS ·

INDEX

A

acoustic torpedo, 17
ailerons, 27
air conditioning, 45
aircraft
  helicopter, 30–31
  jumbo jet, 26–27
airlock, 47
Air-Sea Rescue, 30, 31
anchor, 8, 42
armor plating, 21
astronomers, 6, 7

B

ballast, 8, 11, 42
ballet, 31
  see also opera house
bells, 24
bilges, 9
Blue Riband, 10
body shop, 28
Boeing 747, 26–27
boilers
  ocean liner, 12
  steam train, 35
Britannia, 15
buildings
  castle, 4–5
  cathedral, 24–25
  Empire State Building,
    44–45
  observatory, 6–7
  opera house, 32–33
buoyancy, 16
buttresses, 24

C

cabins
  galleon, 9
  ocean liner, 10, 13, 15
  trawler, 42
cannon
  castle, 5
  galleon, 8, 9
cannon balls, 8, 9
car factory, 28–29
carpenters, 25
carriages
  steam train, 39
  underground train, 41
castle, 4–5
cathedral, 24–25
chimneys
  castle, 5
  steam train, 35
  see also funnels
coal mine, 18–19
conveyors
  car factory, 29
  coal mine, 19
  trawler, 43
cranes
  observatory, 6
  oil rig, 22
crew
  air (helicopter), 30, 31
  air (jumbo jet), 26, 27
  galleon, 8, 9
  ocean liner, 10–15
  space shuttle, 46, 47

steam train, 35–39
submarine, 16, 17
tank, 20, 21
trawler, 42–43
Cunard, Samuel, 15
cutters, 25

D

da Vinci, Leonardo, 20
derrick, 22
drawbridge, 4
drill bit, 22
dungeon, 4

E

electricity
  jumbo jet, 27
  ocean liner, 13
  oil rig, 22
  submarine, 17
  subway, 40
elevators
  Empire State Building,
    44, 45
  ocean liner, 11
  opera house, 33
Empire State Building,
  44–45
engines
  helicopter, 30
  jumbo jet, 26
  ocean liner, 12, 14
  space shuttle, 46
  submarine, 17
  tank, 21
  trawler, 42
escalators, 41

F

factory, car, 28–29
firebox, 35, 36
fishing ship see trawler
Flying Scotsman
  locomotive/train, 34–39
food storage, 8, 12
footplate, 35, 39
fuel, use of
  helicopter, 30
  jumbo jet, 27
  ocean liner, 11
  space shuttle, 46
  steam train, 34, 39
  submarine, 17
funnels, 12

G

galleon, 8–9
galley
  galleon, 9
  ocean liner, 12, 13
  space shuttle, 47
  steam train, 38
  submarine, 17
  see also kitchen
gargoyles, 24
glaziers, 25
Gresley, Sir Nigel, 35
guns
  castle, 5
  galleon, 8, 9
  submarine, 16, 17
  tank, 20

H

Hale, George Ellery, 7
Hale telescope, 6–7
helicopter, 30–31
hull
  galleon, 8
  ocean liner, 14, 15
hydroplanes, 16, 17

I

intelligent pig, 23

K

keel
  galleon, 8
  ocean liner, 11
kitchen
  castle, 5
  oil rig, 22
  see also galley

L

lamp, miner's, 18
lavatories see toilets
lifeboats, 10, 22
lifts see elevators
liner, ocean passenger,
  10–15
locomotive, 34, 35

M

machine guns, 20, 21
Mallard locomotive, 35
masons, 25
mining, 18–19
mirror, telescope, 6, 7
moat, 4

N

Normandie, 10

O

observatory, 6–7
ocean liner 10–15
oil rig, 22–23
OMS engine, 46
opera house, 32–33
orbiter, 46
Otis, Elisha, 44

P

paint
  car, 28, 29
  jumbo jet, 27
  observatory dome, 7
Pan Am jumbo jet, 26–27
payload assist module, 46
periscope, 16, 20, 21
portcullis, 4
Pratt & Whitney PW4256
  engine, 26
press shop, 28
propellers
  ocean liner, 14, 15
  trawler, 43

Q

Queen Mary, 10–15

R

radar
  helicopter, 30, 31
  jumbo jet, 26
  submarine, 16
  trawler, 42
RCS engine, 46
rig see oil rig
road heading machine,
  18, 19
robo-carrier, 29
robots, 28–29
rocket engine, 46
Rolls-Royce Gnome
  turbine engine, 30
roof supports, 18, 19
rotor blade, 30, 31
roughnecks, 22
Royal Opera House,
  London, 32–33
rudder
  galleon, 9
  jumbo jet, 27
  ocean liner, 14, 15

S

sailors, 8, 9
sawyers, 25
Sea King helicopter, 30–31
setters, 25
747 see Boeing 747
shearer loader, 18, 19
ships
  galleon, 8–9
  ocean liner, 10–15
  trawler (fishing ship),
    42–43
shuttle see space shuttle
smiths, 25
soldiers
  castle, 4, 5
  galleon, 8
  tank, 20
space shuttle, 46–47
space toilet, 47
spot-weld, 28
steam train, 34–39
submarine, 16–17, 23
subway station, 40–41

T

T-34 tank, 20–21
tank, 20–21
tanker, oil, 23
telescope, 6–7
tender, 37, 39
theater see opera house
toilets
  castle, 5
  galleon, 8
  jumbo jet, 27
  ocean liner, 13
  space shuttle, 47
  steam train, 38
torpedoes, 16, 17
train, steam, 34–39
transponder
  car factory, 28, 29
  helicopter, 31

transportation
  galleon, 8–9
  helicopter, 30–31
  jumbo jet, 26–27
  ocean liner, 10–15
  space shuttle, 46–47
  steam train, 34–39
  submarine, 16–17
  trawler (fishing ship),
    42–43
  underground train, 40
trawler, 42–43
trim shop, 29
tunnels
  coal mine, 18–19
  underground railway,
    40–41

U

U-boat, 16–17
underground railway, 40

V

V-12 engine, 21
VII-C U-boat, 17
ventilation
  coal mine, 19
  underground railway, 40

W

Westland Sea King HAR
  Mk3 helicopter, 31
winches
  coal mine, 18
  helicopter, 31
  trawler, 42
windlass, 42
windows
  castle, 5
  Empire State Building, 44
  ocean liner, 13
  stained glass, 25

Acknowledgments

Dorling Kindersley would like
to thank the following individuals
and organizations for their help
in the preparation of this book:

Janet Abbott
Ann Baggaley
Boeing International
  Corporation
BP Exploration UK Limited
Tom Booth
Lynn Bresler
British Coal Corporation
British Interplanetary Society
Cunard Line Limited
Agnibesh Das
Robin Kerrod
Kit Lane
London Underground Limited
Dr. Anne Millard
The Science Museum
Andrew Smith
Martin Taylor
Westland Group plc